INTO THE FIRE

Disaster and the Remaking of Gender

In August 2003, one of the largest wildfires in Canadian history struck near Kelowna, British Columbia, and the surrounding Okanagan Valley. The fire covered over 25,000 hectares and the devastation was unprecedented: millions of dollars in property were lost, 26,000 people were forced from their homes, and much of the historical and natural landscape was destroyed.

Environmental disasters occur with increasing frequency around the globe. The enormous consequences of these catastrophes are well documented, especially the economic, human, and physical tolls that are wrought on the stricken communities. *Into the Fire* looks at the social and political dimensions of disasters – including social inequality, power relations, and possibilities for change – focusing on the Kelowna fire and how gender relations were simultaneously sustained and disrupted among those who fought the fire. Shelley Pacholok demonstrates that crises like this provide fertile ground for studying many aspects of social organization, as well as challenge common assumptions and ideologies related to gender. Drawing on media accounts and interviews with firefighters, Pacholok examines not only the experiences and portrayals of male firefighters, but also those of women taking on "masculine" tasks and responsibilities such as repair, rescue, and income-generating activities. Thoughtfully engaging yet theoretically sophisticated, *Into the Fire* reveals how disasters bring traditional patterns of gender relations to light and often serve as catalysts for social change.

SHELLEY PACHOLOK is an assistant professor in the Department of Sociology and History at the University of British Columbia, Okanagan.

SHELLEY PACHOLOK

Into the Fire

Disaster and the Remaking of Gender

UNIVERSITY OF TORONTO PRESS
Toronto Buffalo London

© University of Toronto Press 2013
Toronto Buffalo London
utorontopress.com

ISBN 978-1-4426-4691-9 (cloth)
ISBN 978-1-4426-1470-3 (paper)

Library and Archives Canada Cataloguing in Publication

Pacholok, Shelly, 1966–
Into the fire: disaster and the remaking of gender/Shelley Pacholok.

Includes bibliographical references and index.
ISBN 978-1-4426-4691-9 (bound). – ISBN 978-1-4426-1470-3 (pbk.)

1. Disasters – Social aspects. 2. Disaster relief – Social aspects.
3. Women – Social conditions. 4. Women – Psychology 5. Sex role.
I. Title.

HV553.P32 2013   363.34082   C2013-901942-1

This book has been published with the help of a grant from the Canadian Federation for the Humanities and Social Sciences, through the Awards to Scholarly Publications Program, using funds provided by the Social Sciences and Humanities Research Council of Canada.

University of Toronto Press acknowledges the financial assistance to its publishing program of the Canada Council for the Arts and the Ontario Arts Council.

University of Toronto Press acknowledges the financial support of the Government of Canada through the Canada Book Fund for its publishing activities.

Contents

Illustrations

Figures

Table

Preface

Disasters are an increasingly regular occurrence in the global landscape. The Indian Ocean tsunami, the Haitian and Chilean earthquakes, the Tohoku (Japan) triple disaster, Hurricane Katrina, the BP oil spill, the Russian heatwave and fires, and Superstorm Sandy provide but a few examples. The devastating consequences of these catastrophes are well documented, especially the economic, human, and physical tolls that are wrought on the stricken communities. Recent discussions in critical disaster scholarship focus on the *social* causes of disasters, arguing that these events are neither natural nor inevitable but are the result of the political choices made about people, land, and other resources (Mileti 1999; Schuller 2008). Many predict that global warming, rapid urbanization and development, increasing population and wealth, environmental degradation, and neoliberal policy reforms will increase the frequency and intensity of disasters as well as their human and economic costs (Briceno 2009; Brunsma, Overfelt, and Picou 2007; Enarson 2000; Enarson and Hearn Morrow 1998b; Etkin 1999; Quarantelli, Lagadec, and Boin 2006; Wisner 2009). These risks are borne disproportionately by poor people the world over (Beck 2006; Lewis and Kelman 2012). Attending to the social and political dimensions of disasters – including social inequality, power relations, and possibilities for change– is of crucial importance as we turn the page on one of the deadliest disaster years in recent decades. It is to this task that I turn my attention here, exploring the ways in which relations of power and social inequalities are manifested in the wake of disaster – in particular, the possibilities for disrupting the everyday production of gender.

Before proceeding further, I must explain how I came to this rather weighty topic. Feminists have long maintained that personal histories and positionalities necessarily inform the work that researchers do. In the interest of honouring this reflexive tradition, I disclose at this early juncture my interest in disasters as more than purely academic; I have a personal connection to catastrophic events, one that began somewhat serendipitously almost twenty-five years ago.

Black Fridays

Edmonton, Alberta, 31 July 1987

The heat and humidity were stifling; the sky, a greenish hue. The weather was odd, I thought, as I rushed to pack my bags for a weekend trip. I planned to leave after work that day, and as I navigated the freeway traffic on my way to the office, my thoughts turned to the weekend ahead. I was upbeat, carefree, and, like most twenty-somethings, blissfully unaware of my own mortality.

In the early afternoon a thunderstorm watch morphed into a severe thunderstorm warning, and then, at three o'clock, a funnel cloud appeared south of the city. Sequestered in my cubicle and unaware of the ominous forecast, I waited impatiently for the workday to end so that I could commence my long drive. Less than thirty minutes later I was sprinting to the back of the building in an attempt (slightly misguided) to protect myself from what I would later learn was an F4[1] tornado. With only seconds to spare, I dashed into a small office in the centre of the freight dock and scrambled under a desk. I crouched in fear, waiting as one waits for the impact of a bone-breaking fall. Without warning the power went out, leaving the office cloaked in darkness.

The building took a direct hit. As the tornado passed overhead, the roar was deafening – louder than a jumbo jet and infinitely less familiar. The sound enveloped my body, vibrating, pulsing in its intensity, and then there was silence.

When I opened my eyes, I saw only sky. The roof had vanished, ripped from the steel beams, now grotesquely twisted, that had once supported it. Looking down, I saw my coffee cup, somehow intact and clutched tightly in my hand. I gingerly pressed my fingers to my scalp; I could not tell where my hair ended and the mud began. I stood up. My clothes were soaking wet, the fabric impregnated with mud (I remember exactly what I was wearing, right down to my shoes). Bits of detritus were embedded in my skin, but I was not injured. Some of my colleagues were not as fortunate, having been tossed like twigs from the building, trapped under the weight of the roof's steel beams, or wounded by flying debris.

As I tried to make sense of the scene before me, I realized I was not alone. A co-worker who had also sought shelter in the office helped me to scramble through a shattered window. With two colleagues I manoeuvred my way around a broken concrete slab to terra firma. I began to walk away from the building, wading through ankle-deep water and climbing over rubble as I went. The parking lot, now a misnomer, was devoid of vehicles. I quickly scanned the perimeter. My car was nowhere in sight. Live electrical wires lay on the wet asphalt like poisonous snakes. A broken propane line hissed angrily, spewing its noxious fumes into the damp, thick air. I waited there, for how long I do not know. Never in my life have I so desperately wanted to get away from a place. Eventually I was offered a ride in the back of a pickup truck to a nearby residence. In haste I took it.

That day, forever known to locals as Black Friday, Edmonton was left to mourn the deaths of twenty-seven of its residents, twelve of whom had lost their lives in the industrial area where I worked. The tornado left a path of destruction forty kilometres long, indiscriminately targeting industrial buildings and suburban homes, oil tanks, railcars, transit lines, and livestock. People were trapped in and under buildings, hospitals were flooded, electric power failed, and fires burned. All told, the 400 km/h winds caused over three hundred million dollars in losses. Three hundred homes were completely destroyed, and thousands were damaged. While less visible, the psychic scars were equally tangible for some. A handful of my co-workers went on medical leave, some never to return. Others self-medicated with alcohol and other drugs; one could find the solace of sleep only with a radio by her side.

The following week I returned to work, with others who were able, to sort through what remained of the company's documents and equipment. A year later, the organization was housed in a newly constructed building, and life had returned to its normal rhythm. In time, my career goals shifted, and I moved on to graduate school, but the tornado stayed with me. It will always be part of my personal biography, a piece of who I am. To this day my pulse quickens in fierce summer storms.

Okanagan Valley, British Columbia, August 2003

More than fifteen years later, during a family visit to the Okanagan Valley, a forest fire broke out on the south end of Okanagan Lake. Each day, with growing unease, my family and I looked south from our vantage point at the flame-coloured sky and the rapidly expanding smoke plume. In a few days the entire valley was blanketed in smoke, and ash fell like snowflakes from the smoke-thickened air. Fire reports became increasingly ominous, each day bringing more disturbing news of the fire's growing intensity. The tally of losses to forest land mounted , and then, less than a week after ignition and fuelled by dangerous 75 km/h winds, the fire razed thousands of hectares of forest and hundreds of houses in a devastating twenty-four-hour run. On this Black Friday the city of Kelowna and its residents reeled in shock.

The media coverage of the disaster was extensive. Scouring the newspaper reports, I found myself predictably dismayed by the losses but also reflexively drawn to the people and their stories. I felt a certain kinship with those chased by the flames, powerless in the face of Mother Nature, and forced to confront their own mortality. Black Fridays connected our lives across time and space.

So it was that two disasters and a brush with death provided the soil in which the seeds of this research were sown. My personal connection kindled a curiosity in disasters, which later became an academic interest in the potential for change generated by such events. As a critical sociologist I have a keen interest in social inequalities, and as a feminist I have a personal and political stake in examining the ways in which gender is implicated in relations of inequality. Disasters reveal hidden power relations (De Wall 2008; Vale and Campanella 2005) and socioeconomic disparities (often tragically), but, by destroying the "matrix of custom" (Prince 1920:20), they also create opportunities for change. In this book I undertake a post-mortem case study of the Okanagan Mountain Park fire, exploring the ways in which the disaster disrupted everyday gender interactions and meanings and the implications this had for social relations and inequalities.

The language is intentionally morbid. The fire exterminated vast swaths of vibrant forest and the wildlife harboured there; the blistering heat sterilized the once fertile soil over which it passed. But the fire also threatened to terminate the customary gender privileges that one group in particular – firefighters – had long enjoyed, and it is to this mortal propensity that I turn my attention.

Acknowledgments

To say that this book is the result of a collective effort is an understatement. I can only briefly describe here the tremendous support that I received while carrying out this work; had I been less fortunate, the journey would have been undoubtedly more arduous.

I am grateful to a number of scholars, each of whom sharpened my thinking in different ways. Tim Curry has a knack for identifying timely and relevant topics and put me on to the idea of studying fire. I also thank him for his enduring sense of humour and for reading early drafts of this work. I am indebted to Townsand Price-Spratlen and Steve Lopez for encouraging me to push my analyses in new directions and for providing innovative suggestions for ways in which to do so. I have shamelessly incorporated some of their ideas here. Steve's incisive, in-depth feedback was particularly important in shaping the concluding chapter and in crafting the findings from the fifth chapter into a journal article. I would also like to thank fellow graduate students and faculty members at the Ohio State University, including those in the Gender Working Group. Gillian Ranson's enduring support and enthusiasm for my work carried me through this project from beginning to end. In particular, her thoughts on the framing of the manuscript and her judicious read of early chapters were invaluable. Tracey Adams, paper discussant at the 2009 Canadian Sociological Association meetings, also deserves mention for getting me thinking about the difference between undoing and redoing gender and what it means for change – ideas that percolated for months and which now appear in elaborated form in the last chapter.

Two anonymous reviewers gave thoughtful feedback on my article "Gendered Strategies of Self: Navigating Hierarchy and Contesting

Masculinities" (2009), which appears in revised form as chapter 5. My thanks go to Wiley-Blackwell for permission to reprint this article and to Ashgate Publishing for permission to use material from "Interviewing Elite Men: Feminist Reflections on Studying 'Up' and Selling Out," in *Studying Up, Stared Down: Challenges in Re-directing the Academic Gaze"* (edited by Luis Aguiar and Chris Schneider, 2012), which appears in the appendix herein.

Later versions of the manuscript profited from the efforts of two anonymous readers who offered feedback on everything from my arguments to the prose. Their provocative and sophisticated insights were instrumental in moving the book forward and in linking it more closely to the field of disaster studies. This book is so much the better for their guidance. I also thank the editors at the University of Toronto Press, Virgil Duff and Doug Hildebrand, and the reader on the press review committee for enthusiastically endorsing the manuscript.

I am further obliged to a host of colleagues who exhibited a keen interest in this project. Fellow faculty members at the University of British Columbia (Okanagan) regularly enquired about my progress, provided press-related advice, and listened patiently to my endless questions. My friend and colleague Ilya Parkins generously doled out warm words of reassurance at just the right moments. While I was on sabbatical, the Centre for Research on Life Course and Vulnerabilities (LIVES) at the University of Lausanne, Switzerland, gave me a collegial home base and the necessary time to complete the manuscript. Special thanks go to co-director Laura Bernardi for ensuring that my stay was an intellectually stimulating one, and to my tireless mentor, Anne Gauthier, for galvanizing her extensive academic connections so that my sabbatical plans could come to fruition. I have also had the incredible good fortune of connecting with leaders in the field of gender and disaster whose cheerleading efforts strengthened my resolve to get masculinities more firmly situated on the radar of disaster researchers.

Deep gratitude is expressed to my loved ones who nurtured my spirit throughout this journey. A big hug goes to each of my family members for their love and support, for reminding me of the important things in life, and for regular doses of levity. I am especially indebted to my parents for providing my first interview contacts, food, lodging, transportation, and every other kind of assistance imaginable during my fieldwork.

Writing can be isolating work, and I thank my friends for luring me out of my writing cave into the world of the social, for providing nourishment when I needed it most, for putting up with my disappearing acts when deadlines took priority over everything else, and, above all, for the laughs.

Words cannot do justice to the contribution of my partner, Trevor, who bore at length my single-minded focus, periods of stress and self-doubt, and need for solitude. Thank you for your patience, your sacrifices, your sensibility, and your capacity to love without question or judgment.

The fieldwork for this project would not have been possible without the financial support of the Social Sciences and Humanities Research Council of Canada. A UBC Okanagan Publication Production Grant provided financial support for the index. The top-notch photographs are courtesy of photographers Evan Batke and Cory Bialecki who kindly agreed to share their work.

Finally, as Elaine Enarson graciously observes, "The greatest debt of all researchers, of course, is to those who say yes when we ask for their time and ideas" (2012, x). In this spirit, I thank all of the research participants who volunteered their time, shared their fire experiences, and responded without complaint to my probes on sensitive personal topics.

INTO THE FIRE

Disaster and the Remaking of Gender

1 Black Fridays

Life becomes like molten metal. It enters a state of flux from which it must reset upon a principle, a creed, or purpose. It is shaken perhaps violently out of rut and routine. Old customs crumble, and instability rules. There is generated a state of potentiality for reverse directions.

(S.H. Prince, *Catastrophe and Social Change*)

There was no sun on the day I made my first trip to the regional forestry office. Known for its hot, arid summers, the Okanagan Valley in British Columbia was uncharacteristically cool that year. As I started my two-hour commute, I wondered what the day would hold. Since it was overcast and chilly, the possibility of new fires was diminished, and the chance of finding firefighters at their base was reasonably good. After two weeks of interviews and fieldwork elsewhere, I had become accustomed to last-minute schedule changes and to empty offices, the firefighters having been called to a fire or another emergency. On this day, however, everything started smoothly. Shortly after ten o'clock I arrived at the base, doughnuts in hand, and was relieved to find people milling about. I chatted briefly with the office assistant and a forest protection officer whom I had interviewed several days earlier.

A few minutes later Jack,[1] a long-time veteran of the forest service, arrived and announced that he was ready to start our interview. I followed him to his office, a space that was overflowing with an eclectic array of photographs, posters, prank gifts, and fire manuals, and he proceeded to explain the importance of humour for workers' morale. We talked for more than two hours. Through laughter and tears he described the personal costs associated with his line of work and highlighted its various technical and organizational aspects. He also talked at length about the Okanagan Mountain Park fire,[2] relaying the sequence of events, the public perceptions and misperceptions of the fire, the personal toll on firefighters from the large losses, and the lack of recognition of their efforts.

Later that afternoon Jack invited me along on a helicopter ride over an area burned by one of the last wildfires of the previous summer. I jumped at the chance, and we quickly walked the short distance to the base. After a brief safety demonstration we boarded. I found my way into one of the back seats and secured my headphones and seat belt. As the rotors reached full speed and we lifted off the tarmac, I felt a surge of excitement and anticipation. We ascended quickly, and as we soared high over Skaha Lake and continued south down the valley, the beauty and ruggedness of the terrain came into full relief. Vaseux Lake glittered below, midnight blue against the ruddy clay and sandstone bluffs that encircled it. Our pilot, in search of California mountain goats, deftly navigated the craft through deep, narrow canyons and precipitous outcroppings. It was difficult to imagine that only twelve months earlier this same valley had been ravaged by devastating wildfires.

In the summer and fall of 2003, wildfires in British Columbia had caused widespread damage to forests, wildlife, animal habitat, homes, suburban neighbourhoods, and tribal lands, damage that was unparalleled in recent decades. From a monetary and safety perspective, the costs were enormous – upwards of $6 million per day in the month of August (Canadian Press 2003). Also, tragically, one air tanker and one helicopter crashed, killing three firefighters. Of the hundreds of fires occurring that year, the Mountain Park fire in the Okanagan Valley was especially destructive.

The Making of a Firestorm

Fire is a natural part of the forest ecosystem in British Columbia (BC Ministry of Forests, Wildfire Management Branch 2010c). It is thought that, prior to European settlement, wildfire burned five hundred thousand to one million hectares[3] of land annually. In the dry interior of the province, where the Mountain Park fire occurred, low-intensity fires once swept through on a five- to fifteen-year cycle, preventing ground fuels[4] from accumulating to the point where they could cause more intense, less suppressible wildfires (Keller 2002). When the BC Forest

Service was established in 1912, it emphasized the prevention and control of forest fires. The success of these fire-suppression efforts significantly reduced wildfires (Filmon 2004) and the number of hectares burned. The average number of hectares burned annually during the period from 1994 to 2002 was 25,177 (BC Ministry of Forests, Protection Branch 2006j). However, aggressive fire suppression has concomitantly resulted in a dangerous build-up of forest fuels, tree encroachment on grasslands, and the infilling of the once open, dry forests in the southern interior region of the province (BC Ministry of Forests, Protection Branch 2006i). According to Freake and Plant (2003, 14–15), "professional foresters had predicted that a catastrophic fire would engulf Okanagan Mountain Park. The 10,000 hectares of forest had been left in their natural state untouched by fire for almost 50 years. The forest floor was covered by tinder. Blocks of standing dead trees grew bigger because falling them in BC parks is forbidden. Insects killed many of them, providing more fuel."[5]

In addition to fuel, weather and topography determine a wildfire's progress (Filmon 2004). Dry, hot weather rapidly increases the danger of wildfires (BC Ministry of Forests, Protection Branch 2006b), and the summer of 2003 was extremely hot and dry in the interior region of British Columbia. Kelowna registered the driest June–August period since data were first logged in 1899 and set a record with forty-four consecutive rainless days (Environment Canada Weather Summary, cited in Filmon 2004). One informant noted that the city had less precipitation in the months leading up to the fire than had Death Valley in the Mojave Desert.

The 2003 fire season was one of the most catastrophic in British Columbia's recorded history. Owing to the extended drought in the southern half of the province, forest firefighters faced conditions never before seen in Canada. Lightning strikes, human carelessness, and arson all contributed to the ignition of nearly 2,500 fires, involving more than 10,000 firefighters and support personnel, and burning more than 265,000 hectares, at a cost of $375 million (BC Ministry of Forests, Protection Branch 2006a). A quarter of a billion trees were lost. Three hundred and thirty-four homes, ten businesses, and other valuable structures were destroyed (BC Ministry of Forests, Protection Branch 2006h), and more than fifty thousand people were evacuated. More property was lost to fire than in any previous year in BC history (Freake and Plant 2003; BC Ministry of Forests, Protection Branch 2006a).

Figure 1.1 Kamloops Fire Centre (© Province of British Columbia. All rights reserved. Reprinted by permission of the Province of British Columbia, www. ipp.gov.bc.ca)

Valley of Fire

The province of British Columbia is divided into six fire centres: Coastal, Northwest, Prince George, Kamloops, Southeast, and Cariboo. The Kamloops Fire Centre comprises the shaded area in the accompanying figure. It encompasses 7.5 million hectares and is divided into seven fire zones: Clearwater, Kamloops, Salmon Arm, Vernon, Penticton, Merritt, and Lillooet. The Mountain Park fire occurred in the Okanagan Valley, which is part of the Penticton Fire Zone (BC Ministry of Forests, Protection Branch 2006h, denoted by the arrow.

In 2003 the number of hectares burned and the number of fires significantly exceeded the norm for the Kamloops Fire Centre. The ten-year average for the annual number of fires is 546, while the average for the annual number of hectares burned is 16,298. During the 2003 fire season, 785 fires occurred, which consumed 106,961 hectares (BC Ministry of Forests, Protection Branch 2006h). According to the fire zone manager, a normal season in the Penticton fire zone consists of 120 fires, approximately two of which grow to consume 100 hectares. However, in 2003, 95 fires had already ignited in the zone by the middle of August. In addition, three new fires started on 16 August, and 47 fires were still burning as of that day (BC Ministry of Forests, Protection Branch 2006e).

Two of the biggest fires of the season burned more area than the average hectares *per year* for the entire Kamloops Fire Centre. In addition, seven large interface fires occurred in the Kamloops Fire Centre during 2003.[6]

Disaster Strikes in Okanagan Mountain Park

After decades of fuel build-up and several consecutive years of unusually hot, dry weather, the interior area of British Columbia was ready to explode. A lone spark could start a large, destructive wildfire (Freake and Plant 2003), and that is exactly what happened in the early morning hours of 16 August 2003. Lightning struck in a remote section of Okanagan Mountain Park at 1:55 a.m. at a point about two hundred metres above Okanagan Lake.[7] The fire was located on the east side of the lake in an area of the park that was inaccessible by road.

Jack was on field response duty that fateful day and was the first forest protection officer to arrive on the scene. At 2:30 a.m. he had received a call from the lookout: "We got one in the park." Jack looked out of the window in the direction of Okanagan Mountain Park and decided that he should drive over and check it out. By 3:00 a.m. he was on the scene, taking pictures, evaluating the topography and the fire activity, and deciding what to do next. The fire encompassed about five hectares and was located in steep, rocky, and poorly accessible terrain. He concluded that it was too dangerous for crews to cross the lake (the only way to get to the fire) and climb the steep bluffs in the dark. He requested early morning action by aircraft and firefighting crews, and by 6:30 a helicopter was bucketing the fire. By 7:00 a.m. the fire size had reached about fifteen hectares.

While Jack was assessing the fire from a different helicopter shortly after 6:30 a.m., a local logging company radioed to say that there was another fire, at nearby Ratnip Lake. He flew over the fire and decided that it was more ominous than the fire in Okanagan Mountain Park; it was closer to the city of Kelowna, had continuous fuel and plenty of dead pine beetle trees, and was about 3.5 kilometres from a local tourist lodge. He knew that he had to take immediate and aggressive action. On the positive side, it was more accessible than the Mountain Park fire, the topography was such that heavy equipment could get in, and there was a pumpable water supply. Crews managed to contain the Ratnip fire at just about four hectares, a successful save by wildland firefighting standards.

Meanwhile, the Okanagan Mountain Park fire was proving to be a serious challenge. Ground crews and aircraft were battling wind, heat, dry conditions, smoke, and difficult terrain. Ten to twelve hours after the fire had begun, it took a major run. Gusts of wind played havoc with the flames. Heat and extremely low relative humidity eventually overcame the effects of the water bombers. Two fire spots appeared north of the main fire within fifteen minutes. Two helicopters bucketed these spots immediately but reported that even with a two- to three-minute turnaround they could not make progress, owing to the dry conditions. Pilots dropped water, and by the time they returned from the lake with another bucket, the fire had regained its intensity. By mid-afternoon it was clear that the danger potential of the fire had increased dramatically. Jack received a call from the supervisor in charge of the firefighting operations on the south side. "I remember when he called me. He said, 'Hey, you better come have a look at this, Jack; it's gone.' And from there it's history."

The fire grew progressively larger over the next few days, and on 19 August it took a significant run to the south. The fire expanded from approximately two thousand to nine thousand hectares, pushed by strong winds from the north. On 20 August, Jack's colleague, Robert, working on the south side of the fire, undertook a harrowing burn-off operation in an attempt to slow the advance of the flames. After an all-day struggle his crew managed to save the homes in the small community of Glen Fir:

> We started up at first light, and I told the guys that they had until noon to get the [fire] guard in because I wanted to take advantage of the winds ... So again the fire was still coming back against the wind, and it was

burning still towards Glen Fir and the houses there. We managed to get the guard in; we finished it by about one o'clock ... The reason you put in a guard is you want a starting point. You want something that the fire isn't going to cross ... They did, I don't know, eight or nine kilometres of guard ... Then we came in in the afternoon and we lit it up, and it burned, burned off that whole hillside. So seven, eight hundred hectares ... that's big, very big ... The fire was still moving; even with that, the fire was moving south to the houses. And it was probably within three hundred metres of that one house when we started lighting it.

By 21 August the fire, now thirteen thousand hectares, threatened the city of Kelowna. Homeowners in affected areas were given evacuation orders. The fire threw burning embers up to one hundred metres in front of the main fire. Wildland and structural firefighters, pilots, and heavy equipment operators toiled through the night. Their efforts saved seventeen homes, but twenty-one structures were lost to the flames.

BLACK FRIDAY, 22 AUGUST 2003

By 22 August the five-day-old fire was raging out of control, growing to seventeen thousand hectares in size. Crews continued to construct fire-guards and conduct structure protection, but some firefighters had been pulled off the fire line that afternoon owing to safety concerns. At 4:45 p.m. the fire blew up, pushed by seventy-five kilometre per hour winds and gusting downdraughts. It was moving along three fronts, gener-ally expanding to the northeast with rank-five and -six fire behaviour.[8] The fire's intensity carried burning debris (the size of dinner plates) for six to eight kilometres from the main fire. Wildland fire crews worked alongside structural firefighters to save as many structures as possible. Air tankers, water bombers, and helicopters provided support from the air, and heavy equipment continued suppression efforts on the ground. Unfortunately the winds did not subside until 3:00 a.m. on August 23, and hundreds of homes were lost to the flames.

The Mountain Park fire was what firefighters call a "home-run" fire. As one veteran explained, "there's certain fires that we call home-run fires ... It doesn't matter what you do; the fire, the ball, is going out-side the park." These fires are essentially unstoppable, and firefighting efforts are largely reduced to damage control. As a result, they cause widespread devastation to property and natural resources. The Moun-tain Park fire was no exception. Greg, a long-time member of the for-est service, remarked that he had never seen such fire behaviour in his

Figure 1.2 Mountain Park fire (photograph by Cory Bialecki)

twenty-five years of firefighting experience: "I've never seen a fire do that, ever: just walk above the treetops, one hundred, two hundred feet above the treetops, and kilometres long. Just chewing up, just burning up timber."

The Aftermath

The final size of the fire was 25,912 hectares. The devastation was unprecedented and forever changed the landscape and history of the Okanagan Valley. The fire was described by the Ministry of Forests as "the most significant interface wildfire event in B.C. history" (BC Ministry of Forests, Protection Branch 2003). In the end, millions of dollars of property were lost, twenty-six thousand people were forced from their homes (Canadian Press 2003), a majority of the historic Kettle Valley Railroad trestles (Heritage B.C. 2004) were burned, and virtually all of Okanagan Mountain Park (CHBC 2003) was scorched by the flames, all of which resulted in a state of emergency. Dejected, the city fire chief remarked, "Last night was probably the roughest night in Kelowna firefighting history I would say. We got hammered pretty good. These losses are staggering" (Canadian Press 2003).

Gender Relations in Times of Crisis

A disaster in every sense of the word, the Mountain Park fire is widely considered to have been one of the most severe and destructive interface fires in Canadian history (Sandink 2009). Millions of dollars of natural resources were lost, a significant portion of a national historic site perished in the flames, thousands of people were displaced from their homes and workplaces, and over 250 houses were burned to the ground. Clearly, the Mountain Park fire was a dramatic and harrowing event for all involved, but what is it about this event that makes it interesting to the study of gender? Specifically, how can a crisis of this nature reveal the workings of gender inequality and the possibilities for change? In short, because gender is usually invisible. It is enacted more or less automatically in day-to-day interactions; it is a regular, ongoing, and taken-for-granted activity or, in the words of West and Zimmerman (for example see 1987), a routine "doing." Precisely because it is habitual, much of the work of "doing gender" is taken for granted and thus made invisible (Martin 2001; Pullen and Knights 2007).

The postmodern turn in gender theorizing has had far-reaching effects, not the least of which is a call for greater attention to the ways in which gender is destabilized or "undone" (Butler 2004; Deutsch 2007, 13). Yet the unremarkable, mundane nature of gender interaction makes it a particularly inhospitable phenomenon for investigating fluidity and change. Postmodernism has effectively shifted the focus away from gender stasis and reproduction to fragmentation and instability (for example see the work of Butler 2004 and Lorber 2005), but the mechanisms of change are still unclear. For instance, which conditions are more likely to precipitate or to stymie gender change? How do we know gender change when we see it? And what happens when gender accomplishment cannot be taken for granted – when gender requires more effort to sustain? In other words, what happens when the day-to-day doings of gender are disrupted? Do gender relations change? If so, in what ways?

Crisis events, like the Mountain Park fire, provide fertile ground for studying gender instability and change, or "undoing," because they are precisely the kinds of occasions that have the potential to disrupt the largely invisible doings of gender. Disasters are dramatic and compressed in time, making social processes especially visible and amenable to social research (Fothergill 1998; Tierney 2007). Susanna Hoffman (1998, 56), an anthropologist who lost her house in the 1991 Oakland firestorm, draws on architectural imagery to make exactly this point: "To use, I think, an apt metaphor, in the starkness of disruption as a people recover and reconstruct, they expose the foundations of their cultural structure, the framing of their ties, the joists beneath their cultural character, the divisions by which they organize space, time, and objects, the doors of their conflicts, and the elevation of their ideology. All of it lies open to the ready observer."

Disasters enable us to "see" better how social life is organized, including the everyday accomplishment of gender. Crises also trouble taken-for-granted assumptions and ideologies (Shibutani 1986) and, by their very nature, are unpredictable. Therefore, situations arise that interfere with regular activities and interactions, which can make it difficult for actors to draw on their usual practices for accomplishing gender. For instance, women may take on formerly "masculine" tasks and responsibilities such as repair, rescue, and income-generating activities. This may shift the attitudes about the capabilities of women and improve their position in their households (Bradshaw and Linneker 2009). Therefore, the extreme conditions caused by disasters can both reveal the mundane nature of gender and provide opportunities for transformation.

Apart from these empirical considerations there are theoretical reasons to believe that disasters can generate gender change. Disasters have the potential to generate "crisis tendencies," contradictions that destabilize current gender patterns (Connell 1995, 84). For example, there is a tension between the fact that, on average, men earn higher incomes than do women and generally have better career prospects, despite the massive influx of women into the paid labour force. Women have an interest in changing this pattern of gender practice and have attempted to do so in various ways (for example, trade union involvement) (Connell 1995, 2009). Crisis tendencies like these open up possibilities for shifting such gender relations; at boundaries and points of change, gender dynamics become open to explicit negotiation (Arendell 1997; Legerski and Cornwall 2010), and the seeds of gender change may flourish. It is also possible that disasters can generate precisely the kinds of instability that create these catalysts for change. This book examines one such moment in gender relations, a time when men and masculinity were literally and figuratively under fire, owing to crises in the formerly all-men and highly masculinized occupation of firefighting.

The question of how to go about investigating gender doing and undoing is not simply theoretical. One must determine first whether certain kinds of events make the largely invisible process of gender accomplishment more overt and, second, whether they provide opportunities for gender disruptions to take hold. A crisis, like the Mountain Park disaster, is precisely the kind of occasion that provides a window into the inner workings of gender. The events surrounding the Mountain Park fire created three crisis tendencies (what might be termed *hot spots* in firefighting nomenclature) that had the potential to undermine the ways in which firefighters accomplished gender at work and, ultimately, to destabilize the institutionalized patterns of gender relations, or "gender regimes" (Connell 2000a, 29), in firefighting. The first was widespread damage to property and valuable resources; the second, a hierarchy between firefighting groups; and the third, the presence of skilled women firefighters.

In the pages that follow I undertake in-depth case studies of each of these gender hot spots – these crises within a crisis – analysing firefighters' narratives to assess the extent to which these tensions destabilized gender relations in firefighting. Crisis tendencies like these open up possibilities for change in the structure of gender relations, but they also emerge on a smaller scale (Connell 2009), and it is on this micro level that I focus here. For each crisis I ask, How did firefighters navigate this crisis? Specifically, what strategies did they use to deal with this challenge to gender relations? Did their efforts further entrench gender inequality or did they open up possibilities for new patterns of gender practice? Under which conditions did their strategies result in gender change and stability? And, finally, what constitutes gender change?

Structure of the Book

In chapter 2, I discuss the nuts and bolts of the research methods used in this case study and provide a brief overview of the theoretical considerations and concepts of relevance to this case. In chapter 3, I describe the occupational and organizational milieu in which firefighters labour. The crises generated by the Mountain Park fire took place in the shadow of firefighting's long and dubious history of gender, sexual, and racial exclusivity and in the context of highly masculinized workplace cultures. This chapter will provide readers with a sense of the social and political backdrop against which the fire crises played out and in which the firefighters' gender negotiations took place.

In chapters 4, 5, and 6, I look at gender hot spots: a home-run fire; the disparities in status, recognition, and rewards; and working with women.

Home-Run Fire

When disasters occur, the public looks to emergency responders to stop, control, or at least minimize damage. These imperatives are reflected in firefighters' occupational cultures. Firefighting is an occupation in which "good" firefighters are able to control or exterminate fires and in which success is synonymous with preventing losses to property and other valued resources. Until the fire season of 2003, BC's firefighters were relatively successful at these tasks; in their words, they were used to "winning."

Unfortunately the Mountain Park conflagration proved far too large and intense to decisively control, especially in the initial stages. This home-run fire was difficult, if not impossible, to stop; nevertheless, most firefighters felt that they had lost the battle and had failed to fulfill their protection mandate.

Firefighters' occupational selves are bound up with their duty to protect people, homes, and forest. Moreover, culturally sanctioned masculinity is embedded in the meaning and practice of firefighting work (Chetkovich 1997; Desmond 2007). Therefore, the inability to live up to the standards of good firefighting also presented challenges to masculinity construction. In short, "losing" troubled the link between masculinity and firefighting. This created a crisis tendency in the gender regime of firefighting that created opportunities for the undoing of gender.

In chapter 4, I examine the possibilities for gender change created by the losses and by the firefighters' subsequent sense of failure. I ask, In the wake of the crisis did firefighters reproduce old patterns of masculinity or did their defeat open up possibilities for change? In the case of the former, what strategies did firefighters use to reclaim masculinity? In the latter, what were the mechanisms of gender disruption?

Disparities in Status, Recognition, and Rewards

The Mountain Park fire, and the ways in which local media covered the disaster, created a hierarchy among firefighting groups in which some firefighters became heroes while others who toiled just as strenuously did not. This heightened the tensions around masculinity construction created by losing, as some firefighters felt unsupported and abandoned by the public while others had to prove that they were worthy of their heroic status. The hierarchy also rekindled previously simmering animosities and generated a great deal of combative posturing.

In chapter 5, I ask, Why were some firefighters, and not others, constructed as heroes? How did firefighters negotiate this hierarchy of prestige that pitted groups against one another? What implications did this have for gender relations in firefighting? Were they further entrenched, destabilized, or something else?

Working with Women

The third source of pressure that made the construction of gender problematic was the arrival of women in the formerly all-men domain of firefighting. Their numbers being small, I reserve the bulk of discussion about women firefighters for this chapter. During the fire, men firefighters were required to work very closely with women. For some this was a novel experience. Even most of those who usually worked with a few women firefighters in their ranks had not done so on a large interface fire. So the fire presented a rare opportunity for women to demonstrate their proficiency under very difficult circumstances in the presence of their male colleagues.

Much of the research on gender and work indicates that women's entry into masculinized occupations does little to challenge workplace gender regimes and even entrenches the status quo. Based on this evidence, one would expect that the presence of skilled women firefighters would do little to alter gender relations in their workplaces.

In chapter 6, I argue that this literature paints a partial and somewhat dismal picture of gender relations because (1) it is afflicted by the tendency to use "doing gender" as a theory of gender conformity and, therefore, overlooks the potential for change generated by crisis events, and (2) it gives short shrift to women's agency. It is imperative to further explore the ways in which gender is constructed (and, potentially, deconstructed) in these occupations and to determine the kinds of events that stimulate those disruptions. I investigate what happens when a crisis presents unprecedented opportunities for women to demonstrate skill and competence in highly masculinized spaces. Do their male colleagues continue to accomplish gender in relatively conventional ways or do they rework gender in ways that challenge gender hierarchies? In the case of the latter, under what conditions do women's efforts destabilize gendered patterns of practice? I answer these questions through a close examination of women's agency, namely their efforts to demonstrate their skill and competence, and the implications this had for the construction of gender among their male colleagues.

Losing, receiving unequal recognition, and working side by side with women created openings for gender undoing in the gender regimes of firefighting. However, crisis tendencies like these in no way guarantee the disruption of the status quo and can, in fact, be derailed by actors and institutions that have a vested interest in maintaining the existing state of affairs. So change is never certain, and new patterns of masculinity may emerge that provide new solutions to the problem of patriarchy (Connell 1995). Firefighters' narratives revealed efforts to smooth the rough edges of firefighting masculinities and hinted at the gender tensions in firefighting organizations that had been spawned by employment equity legislation and the normative pressures for gender equality in the world of work. Firefighters had been grappling with new solutions to these "problems" in the years leading up to the fire, and when lightning struck in Okanagan Mountain Park, these tensions were aggravated exponentially. The resulting firestorm caused massive damage to property and resources, and crucially the losses threatened to undermine firefighters' credibility, rupture the link between firefighting and masculinity, and ultimately dismantle the gender regimes of wildland and structural firefighting.

In the conclusion, chapter 7, I reflect on the extent to which these crises disrupted gender and discuss the possibilities for change beyond the gender regime of firefighting. I also consider the implications of my findings for future research on gender and disaster and speculate on which groups will most likely be found at the forefront of progressive gender politics in future disasters.

In the appendix I turn to the politics of undertaking feminist research and explore some of the dilemmas that I faced as a feminist researcher studying gender relations in a rather privileged group of men. Specifically, I discuss the challenges associated with applying core feminist interviewing principles in light of the destabilizing of binaries occasioned by contemporary feminist and postmodern thought. I also consider the ways in which these tensions are connected to issues of quality in qualitative research.

2 Methodological and Theoretical Road Map

Crises provide an opportunity for disruptions in the everyday production of gender. But how does one go about studying the doing and undoing of gender in these moments? What are the methodological practicalities of such an endeavour? Here I discuss the ways in which an empirical analysis of the intractability and malleability of gender can be undertaken, and describe in some detail the methods used in this case study.

Sample Selection and Gaining Access

I began by identifying key contacts through newspaper reports (following Cornwell, Curry, and Schwirian 2003), the BC Ministry of Forests' website, and personal connections with local residents. I invited the contacts to participate in the study and to provide the names of additional firefighters to interview. Along the way it became clear that the media played an important role in shaping the social relations between firefighting groups and in framing the disaster to the general public. As a result, I sought out new participants (for example, media relations people in the forestry department) and contacted previous participants for follow-up questions about the media. I also made a concerted effort to locate women firefighters for interviewing.

During the early stages of this process I was directed to two gatekeepers, one being the Kelowna fire chief. The City of Kelowna's fire department was involved in a lawsuit with a number of insurance companies, and as a result, firefighters were instructed not to talk publicly about the fire. Before interviewing structural firefighters, I met with the fire chief to explain my project, providing him with a list of the questions that I planned to ask and the names of people whom I was hoping to interview. The second gatekeeper was a fire information officer with the Ministry of Forests Protection Branch, who had requested that all invitations for interviews be directed to him. He contacted the people with whom I wished to speak and also recommended a number of participants.

As the Mountain Park fire was an interface fire, several different groups were involved in the firefighting efforts. Four groups fought on the front lines of the fire: structural firefighters, wildland firefighters, pilots, and heavy-equipment operators. All fight fires, but their occupations differ in a number of important dimensions. Structural firefighters are responsible for extinguishing fires in burning buildings; they mainly use fire engines (which pump water through hoses), ladder trucks, and water tenders (which keep water supplied to the fire engines). Wildland firefighters primarily deal with forest fires. There are two types of wildland firefighting groups in this case study: initial attack crews and unit crews. Three-person initial attack crews are usually the first firefighters on the scene of new, relatively small forest fires. They access the fire by truck, helicopter, or aircraft, depending on the location and accessibility of the fire, and then set up water pumps, remove fuel from the fire's path, and dig fireguards to control or extinguish the blaze.[1] Twenty-person unit crews are dispatched to larger fires where significant long-term resources are required. They are responsible for containing the blaze, which includes tasks such as establishing water-pump and hose lines, digging fireguards, removing fuel from the path of the main fire using chainsaws and burning, and securing the fire's perimeter (BC Ministry of Forests, Protection Branch 2006f).

Pilots, as their name suggests, fight forest fires from the air. Helicopter pilots bring equipment to the fire line in slings and drop water or fire retardant from buckets or belly tanks. Air tanker pilots fly various types of planes, which are used to drop fire retardant. An air attack officer, flying in a smaller "bird-dog" or lead aircraft, directs each group. The officer assesses the fire, leads the air tankers to their targets, and dictates their drop strategy (BC Ministry of Forests, Protection Branch 2006g). Heavy equipment operators work closely with wildland firefighters and pilots to contain forest fires. Equipment such as bulldozers, skidders, and feller-bunchers are used to build roads and fireguards, transport water, and fell trees. Pilots and wildland firefighters are employed by the Province of British Columbia through the Ministry of Forests and Range (Wildfire Management Branch),[2] and structural

Description of sample

Firefighting group	Job	Group composition	Gender and number interviewed
Structural firefighters	Fighting structural fires, primarily within the city limits	City of Kelowna firefighters and supervisors	Men (16)
Wildland firefighters	Fighting forest fires, usually outside of the city limits	Initial attack crew, unit crew, supervisors, contract crew, administrators	Men (14) Women (3)
Pilots	Fighting forest fires from the air	Supervisor, air attack officer, air tanker pilot, helicopter pilot	Men (4)
Heavy equipment operators	Fighting forest fires on the ground	Loggers and forest industry employees	Men (3)
Total			40

firefighters are employed by the City of Kelowna. The accompanying table provides a brief description of each firefighting group in the case study sample.

All four groups of firefighters were relatively homogeneous in terms of sexuality,[3] and racial, ethnic, and gender diversity. This was especially true for structural firefighters and heavy equipment operators, most of whom were white men. All the pilots in the sample were white men, although I was told that there were two women employed on a contract basis. Wildland firefighters were a more diverse group. The forest service employs a number of *Native crews* – a term it uses to denote crews primarily comprising First Nations peoples. Two of the men I interviewed were of Aboriginal descent. However, like structural firefighters, pilots, and heavy equipment operators, most wildland firefighters were white. There were also more women working as wildland firefighters, although at the time of the study they constituted only approximately 20 per cent of the firefighters hired each year.

These groups also differ in important ways. For example, wildland firefighters are largely made up of seasonal workers; structural firefighters (not including volunteers) are employed full time and year round; and heavy equipment operators and pilots often work on a contract basis. Wildland firefighting tends to attract students or other young people who have other jobs in the off season; heavy equipment operators usually work in the construction, logging, or forest product industries; and many structural firefighters have a background in the trades.

The sample size of each group reflects the fact that wildland firefighters were the largest group to fight the fire, followed by structural firefighters, heavy equipment operators, and pilots (although the proportions are not directly comparable). The final sample is also a result of participants' accessibility and the theoretical and snowball sampling strategies noted above. As most of the participants were wildland and structural firefighters, my analyses are largely based on firefighters from these two groups.

In any case study there are choices to make about the persons, places, and events on which to focus (Stake 2000). I have explained why it is important to study disaster events and why the Mountain Park fire is a particularly instructive case, but I have yet to discuss the decisions about the participants to include in this book. I chose not to include the narratives of heavy equipment operators, because their primary occupation was not firefighting. Also, while there were three women in my sample, I have chosen to exclude one woman who worked in dispatch, an all-woman setting. I made this decision on the premise that working side by side with men and doing the same tasks present important opportunities for the disruption of gender. These opportunities are not available to women who work in dispatch. It is noteworthy that the dispatcher whom I interviewed appeared to do gender at work on more conventional terms. For example, relaying an incident in which a firefighting crew had missed its check-in call, she described her duties in decidedly maternal language: "We're kind of the mothers in here. We really are. We're like the mother hens, making sure everybody is okay and everybody has their ducks in a row."

I should also note that there were hundreds of women in both paid and volunteer positions who worked many hours during the crisis. However, as in other disaster settings (Fothergill 2004), they were relegated primarily to support roles, such as serving food and finding temporary housing. My sample reflects the fact that there were far more men than women firefighters on the fire line.

Data Collection

In 2004, I travelled to Kelowna to do fieldwork on three occasions. I completed in-depth interviews with firefighters and informal interviews with a number of other people involved in the firefighting efforts (for example, fire centre dispatchers). These interviews took place in a wide variety of settings including coffee shops, outdoor parks, and homes, but the majority were conducted at the participant's place of work. The interviews lasted from just over thirty minutes to two-and-a-half hours, with the typical interview lasting from one hour to one-and-a-half hours. Each interview was recorded using a digital audio recorder. Afterwards I prepared research memos describing the context of the interview (for example, the setting and the comments made by the interviewee before and after the interview) and any observations or preliminary interpretations of important material. I imported these files into a qualitative data analysis software package that I used to store, organize, and analyse the data.

West and Zimmerman (2009, 116) propose that *"any* method that captures members of society's 'descriptive accountings of states of affairs to one another' (Heritage 1984, 136–37) can be deployed for the study of doing gender" (emphasis original). Given this considerable methodological flexibility, why were interviews my primary method of choice? In this case study, I was interested in the ways in which gender was done and undone in and through interactions. Interviews were best suited to illuminate such interactions: firefighters described their own activities and those of their colleagues and how they interpreted these actions. Firefighters' stories, then, provided a window into their workplace interactions.

Firefighters' narratives are also situated in social worlds that exist beyond the interview context; actors draw on cultural discourses to explain their actions and make them understandable to others. Therefore, it was possible to learn about, understand better, and produce accounts of respondents' social worlds by studying the narratives that emerged in the interviews (Miller and Glassner 1997). In this study firefighters' stories revealed the workings of gender relations in their social milieu.

Each interview began with a general discussion of the respondent's occupation and her or his employment history. These questions were designed to elicit contextual information about firefighters' work organizations as well as the ways in which they constructed occupational gender identities. I also asked firefighters to recount their involvement in the events surrounding the fire. These questions revealed the social relations between (and among) groups, as well as the ways in which the firefighters engaged in gender in the context of the fire. I also enquired about the media coverage of the fire, particularly the theme of heroism. Finally, respondents were asked to reflect on whether their lives had changed as a result of the fire and what they learned about themselves from the experience.

Photograph-elicitation techniques (Curry 1986; Harper 2000) were used in many of the interviews, employing pictures of the fire and destroyed homes as a way to facilitate discussion. For the most part, though, I did not ask firefighters explicitly about gender. Relations of power, manifested in and through everyday assumptions and practices – unnoticed and even unintentional – are unlikely to emerge via direct questioning in self-report interviews (Kitzinger 2009). I sensed that I would get the company line or politically correct answers. In addition, I was an undercover feminist, and I did not want to raise any red flags that could potentially disrupt dialogue (see the appendix for an in-depth discussion of this issue). I did probe gender issues in less direct ways by asking firefighters, for example, what made a good firefighter, whether stereotypes about firefighters were true, and why there were few women firefighters. Despite my covert status and the absence of direct gender questioning (in some cases, likely because of it), the mundane workings of the gender order (Kitzinger 2009; West and Zimmerman 2009) – not only its reproduction but tensions and moments of fracture – were revealed in firefighters' talk.

The discursive practices revealed in interviews shed light on social worlds and highlight the symbolic dimensions of gender, but discursive research cannot stand alone. Gender relations are also constituted in, and shape, structural practices, such as the organization of paid and unpaid labour and childcare, that place limits on discursive flexibility (Connell and Messerschmidt 2005; Connell 2001). While attending through discursive interactions to the ways in which gender was practised, I also examined elements of the structural and cultural context in which the fire occurred that both limited and enabled the achievement of gender for firefighters. Specifically, I analysed the organization of the firefighting efforts and the ways in which the print media framed the event and the people involved in it.

In addition, I conducted informal observations at a number of sites including four City of Kelowna fire halls, three branch offices of the forestry department, two air tanker centres, and one helicopter base. In the wait to begin interviews, during breaks between interviews, after the completion of interviews, and during tours of firefighters' work sites I observed the interactions between the workers as well as some of their daily work routines. While on site, I was constantly observing and was able to gather a substantial amount of additional data this way, from mealtime routines to leisure activities.

Analytic Approach

To guide my data analyses and interpretations I drew on constructivist grounded theory (Charmaz 2000) and thematic narrative analysis (Riessman 2008). Although differing in origin, these approaches have tended towards convergence in recent years (Netting 2010), making possible methodological bricolage (Denzin and Lincoln 2000).

Using open and axial coding (Strauss and Corbin 1998), I noted common themes across interviews. During the initial coding I practised the constant comparative method (Glaser 1992; Glaser and Strauss 1967; Strauss 1987) by alternating coding between cases from different groups of firefighters. The themes that surfaced and the comparisons across participants from different groups allowed me to discern the patterns that emerged.

I was also guided by "sensitizing concepts" (Charmaz 2004) from the literature on doing gender, as a way to think about and organize the themes generated from the initial coding process. Grounded theory has been misinterpreted as a strictly inductive method; however, it can be grounded in existing theoretical frameworks while it is able to generate theory (Berg 2001; Strauss 1987). Sensitizing concepts were useful tools for making sense of the data, but I was mindful to remain open to the emergence of new themes as the data analysis proceeded. These analytical strategies of constructivist grounded theory are consistent with thematic narrative analysis, where investigators search for themes across cases, while simultaneously honouring each participant's individual narratives (Riessman 2008).

Mapping the Conceptual Terrain of Gender and Disasters

Social Justice, Disaster Scholarship, and Theorizing Change

There is a long history of scholarship on disasters as moments of opportunity for social change, beginning with Prince's (1920) dissertation on the explosion of a munitions ship in Halifax, Nova Scotia, and later the work of Sjoberg (1962) who asserted that disasters are a "key variable in altering social structures of industrial-urban societies" (356). This thread continued in studies on the dynamics of social and cultural systems in disasters (for example, Form et al. 1956) and in research on community recovery and change (for example, Nigg and Tierney 1993; Hearn Morrow and Peacock 1997). This captivation with change is rooted in the premise that disasters dramatically alter the biophysical environment, and, as a result, adaptation and change are inescapable (Hearn Morrow and Peacock 1997). As the potential for change is embedded in their very fabric, disasters can create "windows of opportunity" for important transformations in political, economic, and social life (Nigg and Tierney 1993, 4). In fact, by some accounts the central meaning of disasters is social disruption (Rodríguez, Quarantelli, and Dynes 2006). As Anne Larabee (2000, 107) offers in her cultural treatise on disasters, there is a "necessary reordering of the world in disaster's wake. As Kai Erickson writes in his study of traumatized communities, the inhabitants experience radical transformations of identity, social relations, and worldviews. The assimilation of disaster is thus a dynamic process of renegotiation with and adaptation to the new terms of existence." Disasters require those affected to navigate new terrain and ultimately to establish a "new normal" (Enarson 2006).

The contours of the new normal, however, are not well known, as empirical findings on post-disaster social change are relatively inconsistent. Some researchers suggest that disasters produce minimal long-term changes; some argue that disasters simply speed up or slow down existing trends; others hold that disasters trigger major social alterations (Hearn Morrow and Peacock 1997; Schuller 2008); and still others maintain that change is uneven, occurring in some contexts and not in others (Davis 2005; Hearn Morrow and Peacock 1997).

Perhaps these inconsistencies are not surprising, given the variation in social systems and networks in different disaster settings, including the socio-political and economic landscape of the affected community; its geographic location and size; and the type, severity. and magnitude of the disaster event. The complex interplay between these variables and broader social change makes it impossible and therefore misguided to seek a single, universal claim about disasters and change. Rather, "differential and contradictory patterns of change are likely to emerge, defying simple positive/negative categorization," and, as such, researchers should focus on the "nature, duration, and extent of these changes" (Hearn Morrow and Peacock 1997, 228; Schuller 2008).

Further, change is not necessarily progressive, as Prince (1920) and a whole host of critical social theorists have pointed out. Post disaster, the new normal is often one in which social inequalities are exacerbated and further entrenched (de Wall 2008). Poor people suffer the greatest losses and receive limited recovery resources (Enarson and Hearn Morrow 1998b; Fothergill 2004; Hearn Morrow and Peacock 1997). The most vulnerable also experience human rights violations (Fletcher, Stover, and Weinstein 2005), disparities in housing and relocation assistance (Ruscher 2006), and diminished social capital (Elliott, Haney, and Sams-Abiodun 2010). Racialized groups are confronted with institutional racism (Henkel, Dovidio, and Gaertner 2006), insufficient insurance settlements (Peacock and Girard 1997), barriers to relocation (Girard and Peacock 1997; Logan 2006), overall declines in the standard of living (Fothergill, Maestas, and Darlington 1999; Button and Oliver-Smith 2008), and social isolation (Klinenberg 2003). As the foregoing illustrates, in many ways disasters further marginalize historically disadvantaged groups.

Few would take issue with the call for researchers, policymakers, the state, and emergency personnel to take responsibility for changing this state of affairs (Lovekamp 2010). There are many possibilities for doing so, including stronger legislation for sustainable development, stricter environmental policies, and altering patterns of consumption. Social scientists have a unique contribution to make in this endeavour by developing a better theoretical understanding of the dynamics of post-disaster change. This, I maintain, is best accomplished through empirical work in tandem with theory development.

The contemporary field of disaster studies is characterized by an applied bent that has come at the expense of theoretical innovation (Lindell 2011). Although social scientific explanation rests on theory, and despite pleas from disaster scholars for further theory development (for example see Quarantelli 2005; Tierney 2007), there has been a failure to incorporate adequate theories of social change into research on disasters (Nigg and Tierney 1993). As a result it is not clear what the catalysts for change are or to what extent disaster-related disruptions result in progressive shifts in social relations. It is now time to move beyond describing patterns of social inequality to ask why and how inequities are exacerbated and ameliorated. One of the key tasks I take up in this book is the development of a theoretically informed understanding of change in the wake of disaster, particularly in the realm of gender relations. Only when social scientists have a better theoretical understanding of these issues can we begin to truly foster a project of social justice.

Gender and Disaster

Disasters unfold in social contexts structured by gender inequality (Enarson and Hearn Morrow 1998b), and a great deal of research reveals the extent to which women are disadvantaged before, during, and after their occurrence.[4] Women's disaster work is often marginalized or discounted (Bradshaw 2001; Enarson 2006), men tend to control recovery resources and are over-represented in positions of authority and leadership (Enarson and Scanlon 1999; Eriksen, Gill, and Head 2010), and women face disadvantages in securing temporary or replacement housing (Enarson 1999b; Hoffman 1998). Disasters also put women at greater risk of domestic violence (Enarson 1999a; Fothergill 1999; Hearn Morrow 1997; Houghton 2009), leave poor women more impoverished (Enarson 2000, 2001), and increase women's domestic labour (Enarson 2001; Enarson and Scanlon 1999; Hoffman 1998). Not surprisingly, after disasters women are more likely to report stress (Reinsch 2009; Tobin and Ollenburger 1999) and to experience additional negative life events (Karanci et al. 1999), a decrease in well-being (Van Willigen 2001), and lower life expectancy (Neumayera and Plümperb 2007). Given women's heterogeneity, some research also considers the ways in which gender intersects with race, ethnicity, class, and age to structure women's disaster experiences and produce or reproduce gender injustice (for example see Enarson and Hearn Morrow 1998b, Fordham 1999, and Luft 2011).

These inequities could lead one to conclude that, although social relations may be temporarily disrupted during disasters, they inevitably revert "back to normal" once the proverbial dust has settled (Alway, Liska Belgrave, and Smith 1998; Eriksen, Gill, and Head 2010), and that gender inequalities are re-established and even magnified by disasters. However, there are also reasons to believe that disasters open up possibilities for progressive change. Since they wreak havoc in the lives of those affected, they create spaces for social transformation – opportunities to build back better political, social, and physical infrastructures (Bradshaw and Linneker 2009, 77). In this vein, scholars have examined the transformative potential of disasters for women's empowerment through grassroots movements (Bari 1998; Enarson and Hearn Morrow

1998a; Enarson 2012; Lovekamp 2010; Neal and Phillips 1990; Horton 2012), finding that disasters can disrupt gender inequality (Bradshaw 2001; Bradshaw and Linneker 2009; Butterfield 2009; Fothergill 2004). All of this suggests that gender relations can and sometimes do change for the better following disasters, but this line of enquiry is in the early stages of development. Thus, little is known about the extent to which disasters foster progressive change or under what conditions (theoretical or practical) this is likely to occur.

Men and Gender Change

Feminists have long debated whether to include men in feminist research, and if so, on what terms, because men's lives, interests, and knowledge have often been foregrounded, while women and women-centred domains have remained invisible (for example see Smith 1987). Some argue that including men in feminist research can illuminate the operation and effects of patriarchy (Price 2010), and others reflect on the extent to which research by or for men constitutes feminist research (for example see Arendell 1997 and Presser 2005). Despite these tensions, there is a general consensus that gender inequality is not simply a "women's issue"; as such, theoretical frameworks and practical solutions must fully consider men as well as women (Kimmel, Hearn, and Connell 2005).

The shift in gender studies to include men has not occurred to nearly the same extent in disaster studies, and gender analyses of men's disaster experiences are woefully lacking.[5] While some have called for more analyses of men and gender relations (Enarson, Fothergill, and Peek 2006; Mishra 2009), for the most part gender continues to signify "women"(Enarson, Fothergill, and Peek 2006). The parallel analytic approach generally constitutes describing gender differences between two fixed categorical binaries, women and men, where the complexity of gender is tamed by a pre-existing normative taxonomy (Valocchi 2005). Scholars have rightfully documented the inequities that women face, but the recognition that gender is salient for both men and women means that it is no longer sufficient to examine women's disaster experiences exclusively (Enarson and Fordham 2001). Further, and foreshadowing the sociological theoretical terrain discussed below, gender is widely conceptualized as a socially constructed relationship, a conceptual complexity that cannot be captured in categorical formulations of gender in which the disaster experiences of women are judged a priori, separate and distinct from those of men.

There are further practical and theoretical reasons to include men (and relations between men and women) in research on gender and disaster. It is the case that men as a group have more power and privilege than have women as a group, in the most general sense. However, there are more sophisticated theoretical tools at hand that enable gender scholars to not only speak of similarity and difference between and among men and women but also consider how the salience of gender is contextually specified. For example, in a "matrix of domination" (Hill Collins 2000, 18) gender intersects with other structures of social inequality, such as race, class, sexuality, and age, to produce multiply constituted subjectivities and social locations in which there are few "pure victims or oppressors" (287). This necessarily requires a rethinking of categorical formulations of gender and patriarchy and problematizes the exclusion of men from feminist-inspired research.

It is precisely in times of uncertainty and crisis – when customary social relations are disrupted – that masculinity is "put on the line" (Morgan 1992, 47) and its performance requires extra effort. Disasters thus provide fertile ground for studying masculinity and gender relations (Messerschmidt 1995; Morgan 1992). Finally, just as for women, normative gender ideologies can have negative repercussions for men affected by disasters when they impair emotional expression, the ability to earn a living, or the ability to otherwise recover from losses (Mishra 2009). These insights suggest that including men in gender and disaster research, as I do in this case study, promises to reveal fruitful insights for the broader feminist project of transforming gender relations. From an applied angle, it also affords opportunities for engaging with men as agents of change (rather than solely as barriers to change) (Mishra 2009).

Theorizing Gender: Patriarchy and Beyond

In these opening pages I have made a case for studying disasters because they necessarily create change (for better or for worse), and I have argued that addressing social inequality requires both a thorough investigation of the ways in which gender is implicated in women's and men's lives. But which theoretical frameworks are best suited to guide such an enquiry? Unfortunately, theoretical work in this area is virtually non-existent. Gender and disaster studies are afflicted with the same malady as is the general field of disaster studies: "long on description and short on theory," as a leading scholar notes (Enarson, Fothergill, and Peek 2006). This can be partially attributed to the focus on policy-related work, which is both important and necessary given the goal of reducing risk and vulnerability in marginalized populations. That said, theory matters; knowledge production has real consequences for the actions of women and men in disasters (Enarson 2012). Therefore, social scientists can and should augment applied work by formulating gender theories that can assist policymakers and practitioners.

Despite the theory lacuna in the field of gender and disaster, there are several broad theoretical approaches on which to build a conceptual foundation for the task at hand.

Patriarchy

Patriarchy is a contested concept, with a variety of meanings and usages in feminist writings. Generally, patriarchy refers to male domination and to the power relationships through which men dominate women (Millett 1969). This binary approach has been criticized by feminists for its inability to account for historical and cross-cultural variations in gender patterns, as well as for ethnic and class differences among women (Walby 1989). Masculinity theorizing points to relationships of domination among men that must also be taken into consideration in any theory of patriarchy (Connell 2005), which I discuss in more detail below.

Marxist feminists have debated the relationship between patriarchy and the capitalist mode of production, resulting in numerous iterations of "dual-systems theory." One such approach draws on psychoanalytic theory to define patriarchy as an ideological phenomenon that is relatively autonomous from social, economic, and historical relations (Mitchell 1974), and subsequent elaborations have focused on gender as constituted through discourses (Beechey 1979). The danger with these approaches, according to some (this author included), is that the material basis of patriarchy (and its consequences) is erased (Beechey 1979; Hartmann 1981).[6] In terms of masculinity, Connell (2005, xix) notes that discursive approaches are limited because they "give no grip on issues about economic inequality and the state ... which are crucial to change in masculinities." According to Young (2005, 494) a feminist theory of gender oppression must "account for male domination as structured in a set of specific, though variable, social and economic relations with specific material effects on the relations of men and women." In this case study, the material dimensions of gender relations have important implications for stasis and change, to which I speak in the concluding chapter.

Gender, Interaction, and Change

Prompted by critiques from feminist post-structuralists and queer theorists, the field of gender studies has attempted to move away from essentialist formulations of gender in which women and men, femininity and masculinity, are conceptualized as fixed, oppositional categories. The vestiges of the essentialist approach can be found in analytic models that operationalize gender as a two-category demographic variable held constant through various statistical techniques in the search for gender differences. Gender scholars of a different persuasion, including some sociologists, draw on a gender relations approach that recognizes the fluidity of gender and the ways in which it is constituted in and through social interactions.

The now classic theory of "doing gender" is one such example. With a distinguished intellectual pedigree, it has been applied in much empirical work. Here, gender is not something that one possesses, like a set of traits or a role; nor is gender fixed prior to interaction. Rather gender is itself the product of social doings; it comes into being in and through social interactions in which actors are accountable to normative conduct for their presumed sex category (West and Zimmerman 1987).

The doing gender approach, with its focus on human agency (Andersen 2005) and the constructed element of gender, contains the seeds for gender change and deconstruction. Despite the transformative potential embedded in this framework, it is largely used as an explanation for gender conformity, with a focus on the ways in which gender difference and inequality are sustained and the gender order reproduced (Deutsch 2007). Deutsch argues that the theory of doing gender renders resistance invisible and makes it difficult to theorize the manner in which gender oppression might be dismantled, in part because the theory is formulated in such a way that renders accountability invariant; whether one conforms to gendered norms or resists them, one is doing gender. West and Zimmerman (1987, 136–7) state: "To 'do' gender is not always to live up to normative conceptions of femininity or masculinity; it is to engage in behavior *at the risk of gender assessment* ... If this be the case, can we ever *not* do gender? Insofar as a society is partitioned by 'essential' differences between women and men and placement in a sex category is both relevant and enforced, doing gender is unavoidable" (emphasis original). Ultimately, Deutsch (2007) calls for a new focus on social processes that resist or subvert conventional gender relations and on a shift from talking about doing gender to illuminating how gender is "undone" in social interactions.

This shift towards fluidity and undoing is also in line with theorizing on masculinity, conceptualized as patterns of practices that create and are recreated by social structures such as gender relations, race, class, age, and sexuality. These patterns of practice are, moreover, historically and culturally contingent. There is not one pattern of masculinity found everywhere, then; rather, there are masculinities (Connell 1995; Kimmel 1994). Some masculinities are deemed culturally superior, hegemonic masculinity being the most honoured or desired at a particular time, in a particular setting; it is the masculinity that is culturally and socially validated. In addition, as a pattern of gender practice that is taken to justify patriarchy, it cannot exist unless there are subordinated Others (that is, women and marginalized men) who are constructed as deficient in some way. Therefore, hegemonic masculinity upholds power and status inequalities, both between men and women and among men (Connell 1995, 2000a, 2000b). This theoretical approach is a significant advancement over the binary conceptualization of patriarchy taken by gender scholars in earlier work.

Crucially, Connell (1995) has long claimed that hegemonic masculinity is not statically reproduced but is always contested and in flux owing to tensions in the gender order; the notion of hegemony implies an "active struggle for dominance"(Connell and Messerschmidt 2005, 832). It is this instability that creates spaces for disruption and change. "Gender relations are always arenas of tension. A given pattern of hegemonic masculinity is hegemonic to the extent that it provides a solution to these tensions, tending to stabilize patriarchal power or reconstitute it in new conditions. A pattern of practice (i.e., a version of masculinity) that provided such a solution in past conditions but not in new conditions is open to challenge – is in fact certain to be challenged" (Connell and Messerschmidt 2005, 853). Crisis tendencies in the gender order mean that hegemonic masculinity is always open to contestation. Masculinities can and do change in the face of challenges (Connell and Messerschmidt 2005), and contemporary gender theorizing must account for this instability or undoing.

What does change actually look like? What, in fact, constitutes a shift in gender relations after a catastrophe? How, for example, will we recognize gender undoing when we see it? Almost twenty years ago Nigg and Tierney (1993) stressed the importance of specifying change in the field of disaster studies, stating that "unless we are more able to define what we mean by disaster *and what constitutes change*, we cannot expect to make much progress in discovering how they are related" (33; emphasis added). My aim in this book is to provide some preliminary answers to these questions through an empirically based elaboration of gender theory. Weaving together the heretofore disjointed threads of masculinities, social change, and disasters, I explore the extent to which gender relations are undone in the wake of disasters. Towards this end, I undertake an in-depth analysis of each of the gender crises that flared up after the Mountain Park fire.

3 Firefighting Is a Man's Game: Organizational Cultures and Practices

As far back as the late nineteenth and early twentieth centuries, structural firefighting was symbolically and numerically a world of men. Public visibility and the nature of the work – fighting the most feared of nature's elements and saving lives and property – meant that the firemen of yore were celebrated as exemplary models of chivalrous and heroic manhood (Cooper 1995). This tradition lives on in the iconic image of the quintessentially courageous, strong, and selfless male firefighter (Childs, Morris, and Ingham 2004; Tracy and Scott 2006).

Wildland firefighters do not enjoy the same cultural prestige (Desmond 2007); nevertheless, the occupational culture has long been a highly masculinized one (Enarson 1984). Wildland firefighters have also begun to garner more public attention in recent years. Several books have appeared in the popular press (for example, *A Season of Fire* by Douglas Gantenbein and the widely read *Young Men and Fire* by Norman Maclean), some of which invoke heroics and bravery to describe firefighters' work (for example, *Wildfire Wars: Frontline Stories of BC's Worst Forest Fires* by Keith Keller and *The Thirtymile Fire: A Chronicle of Bravery and Betrayal* by John N. Maclean).

Despite the different histories, contemporary wildland and structural firefighting can both be characterized as highly masculinized occupations. In terms of gender segregation in Western industrialized countries, typically less than 5 per cent of structural firefighters are women (Lewis 2004). In the United States, 3.6 per cent of structural firefighters are women (US Bureau of Labor Statistics 2010), and in Canada (and British Columbia) the picture looks much the same, with women hovering at about 3 per cent (Statistics Canada 2006b). For wildland firefighters the situation appears slightly more progressive. The British Columbia Wildfire Management Branch does not track the number of men and women in its ranks; however, in 2011 one administrator estimated that women constituted 25 to 30 per cent of the wildland firefighters hired each year. In the broader occupational category of forestry and silviculture workers, women make up 19 per cent in British Columbia (Statistics Canada 2006b) and 13 per cent in the entire country (Statistics Canada 2006a).

These numbers indicate that, by and large, the gender regime in firefighting has been relatively impervious to the challenges created by broader shifts in the gender order. Despite the equal rights movement, the calls by liberal feminists and other groups for women's equal opportunities in the labour market, and the employment equity legislation designed to remedy the under-representation of marginalized groups in various occupational sectors, firefighting occupations were and are mainly populated by men. Also noteworthy is that white men have long been dominant in this realm (Cooper 1995). In Canada 2.5 per cent of structural firefighters are visible minorities, and in British Columbia just over 3 per cent (Statistics Canada 2006b). For forestry and silviculture workers, 2.3 per cent are visible minorities in Canada, and 3.3 per cent in British Columbia (Statistics Canada 2006a).[1]

Given this broader occupational context, it is not surprising that the workplaces of the wildland and structural firefighters who fought on the Mountain Park fire were also highly masculinized. They were characterized by a gendered division of labour, a valorization of stereotypically masculine personality traits and body types, and a mandate for new recruits to fit into the existing gender regime. Both groups also lay claim to masculinities that are, in many ways, consistent with hegemonic masculinity.

In wildland and structural firefighting organizations there were very few women, if any, working side by side with men. In the Kelowna Fire Department's stations all the 100 structural firefighters were men.[2] In contrast, there were a number of women working as wildland firefighters. Each year the Province of British Columbia employs approximately 850 seasonal firefighters, and at the time of the Mountain Park fire roughly 20 per cent of these recruits were women. In the mid-1990s, on the initial attack crew that I studied, all eighteen crew members were men. Two years later two women were hired, and the following year another woman was hired. Since that time they have averaged three women on an eighteen-person crew. On the twenty-person unit crew there were three women and seventeen men in the summer of 2004.

When women were employed in the same workplaces as were men, they typically worked in different types of jobs, which were often characterized as "support" roles. In the Kelowna Fire Department there were no female firefighters, but there were two women in administrative positions and two dispatchers. Similarly, on wildland firefighting bases women were primarily employed in administrative and secretarial positions. In the regional fire centre the upper-level managers were mostly men, and the departments such as dispatch were made up of women. One employee noted that, as far as he knew, no men had ever worked in dispatch. Finally, at the time of the study there was only one woman leader of an initial attack crew in the entire province of British Columbia.

There was also a gendered division of labour on very large fires (also known as *project fires*). When fires burn for extended periods or when the workload is heavy, an Incident Command team is called in. The team comprises an incident commander (responsible for the overall management of the fire); operations (who fight the fire on behalf of the incident commander); finance and administration; logistics (in charge of transporting, feeding, and housing crews); and planning (responsible for fire-behaviour predictions, evacuation procedures, and documentation) (BC Ministry of Forests, Protection Branch 2006c). In the Incident Command hierarchy all of the incident commanders and division supervisors were men. There were also no women to be found in operations; women worked in separate positions in finance and logistics.

In short, firefighters' workplaces could be classified as "safe" places (Dellinger 2004, 550); that is, men were in positions of power, and their workplace cultures strongly supported culturally dominant ideals of masculinity. Firefighting organizations were relatively successful at excluding women from the highest-paying, stable, and most desirable jobs. This is an especially remarkable feat, given that such jobs are scarce in this region of the province and the competition for firefighting positions is stiff. For example, the Wildfire Management Branch receives 1,000–1,500 applications per year on average. In a typical year 550 applicants are interviewed, and only 100–200 of those applicants are hired. Almost 80 per cent of firefighters are recalled from previous years, making for a very small pool of new firefighters each year (BC Ministry of Forests, Wildfire Management Branch 2010b, 2011).

Extinguishing the Embers of Dissent: Differentiation and Keeping Others Out

The crisis tendency created by the discrepancy between broader social ideals of gender equality and the obvious under-representation of women (and marginalized men) in firefighting had, by and large, been successfully defused by the firefighting organizations in this study. The definition of worker in firefighting has been and continues to be male, and it mirrors the pattern of hegemonic masculinity that posits men as the opposite of women and necessarily their superiors. Firefighting discourse reflects this rhetoric and works to construct differences between firefighters and Others. Amplifying or creating differences based on one or more attributes enables privileged groups to set Others apart and define them as inferior, in turn providing "justification" for unequal rewards and the sex-gender hierarchy. This process of differentiation is the primary mechanism through which dominant groups in general, and powerful men in particular, maintain their privileged position (Reskin 1988, 62) and contributes to the maintenance and reproduction of occupational segregation (Charles and Grusky 2004).

Firefighting Masculinities

Firefighters used differentiation in subtle and not so subtle ways to justify the dearth of women in their ranks. First, they constructed firefighting masculinities in ways that channelled hegemonic masculinity, a pattern of practice that commonly excludes women. Structural firefighters, for instance, constructed a shared sense of masculinity through discourses that valorized aggression, physical strength, risk, and bravery – characteristics associated with appropriately gendered men. For example, the interview with this structural firefighter, Mark, was rife with references to helping people in trying and often dangerous circumstances: "Our job as firefighters is to help people in their time of need. You know, everybody says, yeah, when everybody's running that way [away], we're going that way [towards the danger], right?"[3] While Mark would probably deny being a hero (a theme I discuss in chapter 5), at the very least bravery is implied.

Wildland firefighters shared some commonalities with their structural counterparts. For example, they stressed that their work is dirty, hot, dangerous, and physically arduous. Pilots also emphasized danger: "[We] are flying 100 feet off the trees, in smoke, in [rough] terrain, box canyons. It's not for everybody!" Both wildland and structural firefighting masculinities mapped seamlessly onto key dimensions of contemporary hegemonic masculinity. An important exception to this pattern, however, is social class; firefighters are relatively well paid, but they have neither the educational credentials nor the occupational prestige of men working in the corporate world. In the global North, hegemonic masculinity includes the imperative for "clean" (mostly white-collar) highly paid work (Connell 2000a).

Personality and Fitting In

When asked what made a good firefighter, many of the men claimed that it took certain attributes in order to be successful, and these attributes, not coincidentally, fit neatly with cultural ideals of masculinity. For example, having the "right" personality in order to "fit in" was often mentioned, the right personality being type A. Shane, like many of his structural firefighting colleagues, maintained that type A personalities were best suited to the job. When asked to elaborate on these characteristics, he remarked: "I think another good example of [type A personality] is you sort of learn to be aggressive. Like, when you get to a fire, you learn pretty quickly that – like when you're a new guy, you show up and if you hesitate for a minute, someone else, you know, they got the nozzle and they're putting the fire out. I mean, you don't have time when you get to an emergency situation to sit around and figure out what you're going to do. You've gotta know. And you learn that. I think guys sort of become control freaks as a result of that, because you have to take charge and you have to do it quickly." Successful firefighters are those with a type A personality, which includes being aggressive, competitive (if you hesitate, somebody else will grab the hose), and dominant (you have to take charge).

Wildland firefighters also drew on traits consistent with the type A personality to describe successful firefighters. Tom, a former wildland firefighter who had recently moved into an administrative position, lamented recent efforts to remove gender bias in physical exertion tests, alleging that they were too easy and resulted in less physically fit firefighters. Here, despite a nod to diversity, Tom claimed that good firefighters had several important personality characteristics in common: "We do have quite a variety of people on the crew – of personalities, and lifestyles, and everything, but I think the common factor is probably a fairly driven person, obviously someone that can handle uncertainty, someone who can handle long hours, lots of responsibility in high-pressure situations, and you have to enjoy being outside, and you have to enjoy hard work, there's no way around it."

Desired worker attributes are typed as "masculine" or "feminine" (Lorber 2005). Type A personality – an aggressive, rational, competitive, driven over-achiever – is culturally signified as masculine and therefore male. As such, firefighters' discourse works to differentiate between good firefighters and Others, men and women, masculine and feminine. And if good firefighters are masculine men, it only "makes sense" that there are few women firefighters.

Women firefighters (those working as firefighters and those wishing to be hired) are further disadvantaged by organizational mandates for the "right" personality. Hiring processes work to select those with a particular personality, in part because this is viewed as essential for fitting in. Kyle, a junior structural firefighter, explained that the hiring process works to select those with certain character traits: "When you're trying out, the different things that you have to go through – you have to put in an application and they sort through that, and then you have to do a written exam, physical, and then interviews – and it's all funnelling down to that kind of [type A] personality … It's like a cookie cutter. Pretty close. I mean there's one or two guys that kind of, you know, maybe slip through the cracks or whatever, still good guys but just not exactly in that mould, right? But pretty much I think the majority of us are pretty close." Kyle's colleague stressed the importance of the interview for finding people that will fit in: "The way they interview them, they make sure that they do fit in with the rest of us, sort of deal. They know what we're like, sort of deal, so you know they sort of groom it that way."

Kyle also went on to point out that finding a person who would fit in was even more important than the knowledge or skills because those could be taught on the job: "That's the biggest thing, hey? You need someone that fits in. If you got a guy that didn't score very well on the exam, that doesn't matter as much as he's able to fit in with the guys, because you'll be able to teach them on the job."

Importantly, newcomers must also integrate themselves into a highly masculinized occupational culture. One summer afternoon almost a year after the fire, I had a long chat over coffee with a structural firefighting veteran. Grant was an introspective participant and especially observant when it came to workplace gender dynamics, so our conversation was an emotionally charged one. He equated the interpersonal relations of the fire station to "locker-room mentality" – a sports team atmosphere in which weakness is disdained, hierarchy prevails, and newcomers are appropriately deferential. Insightfully, he observed the linkage between these rules of conduct and masculinity: "I guess it probably ties into the macho thing. You know, like … don't show if you're weak, don't show your weakness, know your place, shut up and earn your – you know, shut up until you've been around for a while. 'How long you been here? I've been here for 28 years, and you've been here how long? Like, shut the fuck up.' Right?"

Fitting in was not unique to the structural firefighting setting. A forestry employee indicated that personality was an important consideration because wildland firefighting crews spent so much time together: "A lot of different things factor into our decision in hiring people, and a good portion is personality. Personality is a big thing. Ah, you know, you're working in close quarters with someone in general. I mean, once you establish your crew, the three of you will not leave each other's side for quite some time ... You have to be able to get along."

Employers' preferences for a certain personality type and someone who will get along with his or her colleagues clearly favour a certain demographic. These requirements are most readily filled by a person who has similar characteristics to those already working in the occupation – in the case of these firefighters, primarily white, heterosexual, "masculine" men.

The Physical End of the Job: Essential Differences between Women and Men

Almost all the structural firefighters engaged in differentiation by pointing to physiology, in addition to type A personality, to explain the dearth of women in their occupation (with the exception of Grant, who also identified "locker-room mentality" as a possible deterrent). A self-described chauvinist, Steve gave a common explanation: "Women do apply, but the physical end of the job is where they'd probably break down more – in their shoulder strength; upper body strength is what they really need; then you need leg strength underneath you." This apparent lack of strength is problematic, according to Steve and his colleagues, not only because it is required to pass the fitness test, but because firefighters must have the ability to pull their colleagues out of burning buildings, which is a difficult physical feat, according to most. It is not clear how often this heroic act is actually required; nevertheless, it is used to assert that women are not strong enough to do the job.[4] The linking of bodily capital (strength and physicality) to job competence (Monaghan 2002) draws on and reinscribes a discourse of embodiment in which women are constructed as being different from men and, hence, inferior firefighters. Moreover, constructing women as physically weak and, therefore, unable to do what men do allows firefighters to resolve the contradiction between the presence of women and a corporeal occupational masculinity based on strength, because it suggests that the few women who do manage to succeed are aberrations.

Notably, the maxim of biological gender differences shaped firefighters' talk about their work even in the face of evidence to the contrary. This made it more difficult to maintain the "firefighting is a man's game" narrative, but work to maintain it they did. For example, some structural firefighters who pointed to gender differences in physical strength to explain the scarcity of women noted that they themselves weren't "big" guys. The possibility that their own stature might contradict their assertions about physical strength did not seem to be apparent, because the desire to maintain the narrative trumped contrary evidence.

Others seemed to recognize the contradiction between the "necessity" for physical strength and their own physicality and attempted to explain it away by saying things like "you don't have to be the biggest guy," you "need some guys with brains," and a smaller firefighter is more efficient. One of these men, Grant, who used to think that he could never be a firefighter because they were all "great big, huge guys," argued that someone who was physically fit and average in size was a better firefighter than someone who was physically big, and strong.

> GRANT: I don't think most [firefighters] are great big guys; most of them are in pretty good shape and stuff.
> SHELLEY PACHOLOK: Pretty strong?
> GRANT: Yeah, most of them. Not all of them though. But I think if I can say that the more average-size guy in good shape – I'd rather have a squad or a crew of guys that size than a crew of guys 6'2" and 250 pounds and stuff like that, because the average-size, good shape crew will go a lot longer than those guys will.
> SP: Oh, is that right? Stamina wise?
> GRANT: Yeah, for sure. Because the big guys, I mean they're strong, they're in good shape, but they're carrying an extra lot of weight. And compared to some guys, I don't care what shape you're in, that becomes a burden after a while ... So I think an average size guy in good shape is a more versatile, more effective firefighter in most situations.

While Grant seemed to recognize that his physical size may be viewed as problematic, like most of his colleagues he did not follow this line of reasoning to its logical conclusion: if having a very large physique is, in many ways, a detriment, one should find more women working as firefighters.

The tension between the master narrative of biological difference and the firefighters' observations was not as easily erased for one of Grant's colleagues. Mike, who noted that the fitness test tended to "weed out" women, was also cognizant that there are physiological and other *similarities* between women and men:

> SP: So there's the [physical] test part. Do you think there's anything about the job per se that maybe wouldn't be appealing to women or that might appeal more to men?
>
> MIKE: Well, this doesn't appeal to men I don't think, but the blood and guts and stuff like that in a car accident, I can't see – well, actually no one wants to see that, right? Maybe that part of it, maybe women might have a tougher time with children? Seeing children in trouble or ... like, and that's – I've never seen one and I hope I can go through my whole career without seeing one. Because that's what the guys say is the absolute worst, you know. And maybe they see that, with the maternal thing, and you know, maybe that's a tougher aspect for them. I don't know, I can't speak for women. [He laughs.]
>
> SP: I know and I don't want you to. I'm just puzzled because it really does seem like a good job.
>
> MIKE: Great job.
>
> SP: And I can't figure out why more guys apply than women. So I'm trying to figure out, what is it about the job that would either turn women off or maybe appeal more to men?
>
> MIKE: Well, the men, I don't know, because I mean it is an adrenalin thing as well. When the phones go off, it's – not that you guys don't get adrenalin, but that's where maybe the macho part of it comes in, you know? It's adrenalin, we're going, we're, you know – I don't know. I don't know.

Mike struggled with my questions regarding the gender ratio in his workplace. Earlier he had indicated that most women cannot pass the fitness test but that plenty of men have difficulty too. He mentions "blood and guts" but notes that nobody wants to see that. He says maybe it is an "adrenalin thing" and then observes that women have adrenalin too. He makes a connection between adrenalin and being macho, but earlier in the interview he defined himself as someone who is not macho (or at least someone who is closer to the middle of a masculinity continuum). He speculates that women would have a hard time seeing an injured child (because of their maternal instincts) but notes that it is the worst part of the job, and something that he too hopes never to see.

Mike relies heavily on biological reasons (for example, physical strength, adrenalin, and maternal instinct) to explain workplace gender segregation, but for each explanation he acknowledges conflicting evidence. Mike's dilemma is that the "firefighting is a man's game" narrative relies on differences between men and women; however, this contradicts at least some evidence about gender similarities. While many of his colleagues did not recognize or they chose to ignore contradictory evidence, Mike was cognizant of the contradictions in his account, which he attempted to resolve. However, he was unwilling to forsake the master narrative, which in the end simply left him with "I don't know."

Physical strength was not invoked to any substantial degree by pilots or wildland firefighters. This is likely because there were more women in the ranks of wildland firefighting, and these women were required to pass a physical test. When asked why there were so few women in the profession, Hank, a supervisor in the Ministry of Forests, remarked that it couldn't be the fitness test, because "many women pass that." Pilots do not require recruits to pass a test based on physical strength. The explanations of pilots and wildland firefighters were largely couched in the language of individual choice and personality traits (especially type A personality).

Firefighters' adherence to discourse that posits physical strength and masculinized personality traits as prerequisites for success works to differentiate men from women and, subsequently, "good" firefighters from Others. In short, differentiation provides justification for patriarchy; if men are stronger than women and a better fit in terms of personality, they are clearly better suited to the rigours of firefighting. Therefore, it is acceptable, even desirable, to mostly exclude women and Other men from their ranks (the women who did get in were exceptional).

It is worth noting that the firefighters did not use "Other" to describe women. Rather, I am making the claim that their talk constitutes the act of othering because it is politically motivated. Positioning women as the Other produces a homogenized category that does not map onto the lived experiences of the women whom the firefighters encountered and with whom they engaged. The point of Othering is to impose homogeneity even where it does not exist. Categorizing women firefighters as Others (albeit through discursive indirects) enabled firefighters to more easily exclude or otherwise marginalize them because in this process women were constructed as essentially different from men. While firefighters' talk worked to construct women firefighters as a homogeneous Other, it was clear that there were tensions, contradictions, and diversities in women firefighters' gender practices. In chapter 6, I describe their fragmented and sometimes contradictory nature.

Ultimately, differentiation and othering enabled firefighters and their respective organizations to temper the crisis tendency in gender relations that had been created by the fact that both wildland and structural firefighting continued to be male-dominated occupations despite social mandates for gender equality in the world of work. The small number of women firefighters in wildland and structural firefighting organizations certainly suggests that differentiation was functioning effectively to keep Others out.[5] However, there were also signs that change was afoot.

Distancing from Hypermasculinity

While the firefighters clung (sometimes incoherently) to a master narrative of gender difference, they also attempted to file off the rough edges of firefighting masculinity, suggesting that there were tensions in masculinity construction. Many positioned themselves as keenly aware of gender politics and resisted being typecast as a hypermasculine firefighter.

Structural firefighters largely agreed that they were a "macho" bunch, and appropriate firefighting masculinity was certainly valued and rewarded; however, more than a few structural firefighters disparaged the hypermasculine firefighter, portrayed as a "big brawny guy, who kicks down doors and asks questions later." Many noted that in addition to having physical strength, firefighters should be "caring," "personal," and "able to deal with people." One fire department administrator noted that firefighters "are not as hard as you might think – they have feelings but they don't play that up." Jaime, a structural firefighter supervisor, explained that there was more to the job than putting out fires:

> One thing that we're starting to realize or coming to grips with here is that you don't have to be the 250 pound, you know, muscle guy and dead from the neck up to do this job. There's a lot of the job that takes a lot of intellect, a lot of common sense, a lot of work experience in other places and

the ability to connect with people. Back in the '60s, '70s, that's what the job was. It was kicking the door in and putting the fire out. And there's a lot more to it now. And we're – I think we're trying to prepare our officers especially with the soft skills they need to not only get their crew to perform to the maximum on the job, but also when they go to – out in the street and they're dealing with the public in the worst case scenarios, to make a connection ... and to show compassion and to show we care, and we're here to help you.

Charlie, also a veteran firefighter, acknowledged the importance of "soft" characteristics. When asked whether he felt that the firefighter stereotype was accurate (that is, emotionally and physically strong, aggressive, manly, tough), he replied:

> It is, to a degree, but I think you still have that soft, caring side. I think you have to have that otherwise you wouldn't be able to do the things you do to help people. You know what I mean? ... Now firefighting is becoming more technological and scientific in ways. It's not just the big-guerrilla-type guy who kicks the front door down and goes in the house and puts the fire out anymore. It's a lot more mechanics and science to it. And the training and education that we take and do is way more ahead and advanced than it used to be years ago. A long time ago firefighting was kind of like a low-paid, kind of "oh, you can't do anything else, so be a firefighter" type job. It used to be that way a long time ago. But it's slowly – it's become more, a bit of an esteem kind of job, you know? People kind of put you up there a little more than they used to.

Both Jaime and Charlie, and a number of their colleagues, stressed the importance of soft skills and caring, traits commonly associated with femininity. In addition, they emphasized that their job required more intelligence, training, and skill than it once did. This rhetorical shift effectively distances them from the "muscle," "guerrilla" guy of the days of old who is derisively positioned as intellectually inferior.

These dynamics illuminate important gender tensions in the narratives of structural firefighters. The majority dissociate themselves from the lowly, physically large, and strong firefighter who is "a little thick between the ears" and construct their workplace masculinity in a way that emphasizes skill, rationality, intelligence, and caring. Their narratives imply that brute strength is not as important as it once was and that it actually might be something to be disparaged, associated as it is with lesser mental capacity (and, by some, with less efficiency). This talk signals a more enlightened and modern kind of man. Further, the talk of firefighting as more scientific and rational and less brutish mirrors the broader push to professionalize and modernize structural firefighting, to reframe it as clean, white-collar work (Childs, Morris, and Ingham 2004) deserving an appropriate dose of middle-class respect.

The advantages gained by these strategies, however, make the master narrative of biological gender difference logically inconsistent as they suggest that hypermasculinity and brute strength are no longer requisites for successful firefighting. The logical implication is that Others (read, women and less "manly" men) can do the job just as well. Nevertheless, almost all the structural firefighters drew on the ideology of gender differences in physical strength to explain the scarcity of women in their occupation. In effect, their discursive strategy – divorcing themselves from the hypermasculine stereotype – backed them into a corner, making it somewhat illogical to draw on physical strength to explain the lack of women. However, because they had to justify patriarchy if they were to maintain the homogeneity of their organization, many seemed unwilling to recognize this flaw in their reasoning.

Like the structural firefighters, the wildland firefighters associated excessive masculinity with lack of intelligence; they attributed both traits to their American counterparts, from whom they distanced themselves. Many wildland firefighters indicated that there were some "fundamental differences" between Canadian and American wildland firefighters. Tom, who had recently moved into an administrative position, had worked with wildland firefighters from the United States during his time as a wildland firefighter. In his opinion, Canadian wildland firefighters were more experienced, highly trained, and safety conscious. In contrast, he portrayed American wildland firefighters as hypermasculine, with a reckless disregard for safety:

> TOM: In Canada – and this is the way procedure works with air drops – the bird dog will come through, run a siren, let you know he's coming; you're in communication. You clear the path, the drop path. The tankers come in, do their drops; we move back in. That's the way it's supposed to work. In the States it's a badge of honour to be painted. We call it being painted by flame because the red retardant makes it look like you've

been painted. So they consider that a badge of honour if you're in the middle of the drop.

sp: Can't that stuff kill you if it lands on you?

tom: It's heavy, and if you get a full load from an Electra [aircraft], it can kill you. So I've heard direct accounts from air attack officers who will run, go do the all clear – "Everyone's all clear?" "Yup, we're all clear. We're all clear" – come through the final run, and just as [the bird dog is] passing over, the tanker's right behind him about to do his drop, and he can just see people running underneath the path so they can get hit. And I was down there [on a fire] ... and we're down there eating our dinner at the end of the day, and this guy just comes strutting in. He's painted from head to toe in this sticky red crap that itches like hell; it rots your shoelaces, it's brutal stuff. [In a gruff voice:] "Yeah, got painted today, yup, yup, yup." You know, I was down there for five minutes, and already the Vietnam War was being referenced. And it's like, pal, we don't have guns, we're not shooting people, we're here to put out fires. It's just that general attitude, you know: I'm gonna get in front of that thing and I'm gonna stop it, no matter what!

Wildland firefighters also viewed themselves as far more modest than structural firefighters; they are not the "macho 911 saviours of everything" or the type to "jump in front of a camera."

Firefighters' efforts to differentiate themselves from hypermasculine stereotypes suggest that the gender terrain in firefighting organizations was beginning to shift away from the traditional patterns of firefighting masculinity to the construction of more socially progressive, caring, and safety-conscious firefighters. I reserve discussion of the gender politics informing this construction for the concluding chapter.

The Level Playing Field

Tensions in masculinity construction were also evident in the firefighters' attempts to soften the hard edges of firefighting masculinity. Structural firefighters did so by claiming that they were happy to "let" women in as long as it was on equal terms. Many maintained that women were welcome in their occupation as long as they did not receive any special treatment in the hiring process; the competition for jobs must be played on a "level playing field." Somewhat ironically, Norman invoked this metaphor while acknowledging that women were at a disadvantage because most did not have a background in the trades (an attribute that earned extra points in the hiring process):

> There's a few guys in the department and they're kinda your "Oh, we don't want women around here' [in a gruff voice], you know, kind of thing. That's the way they are. But, you know, the majority of guys have got the attitude that so long as they're not hired strictly because they're female, they have to make the same requirements and go through the same testing. You know, it has to be a level playing field. And so long as that – if there's a woman that comes along that can do the same, by all means hire her. But that's not always the way it is across the board. Um, like, down in the States, women – there's two tests, like when it comes to the physical part of the test: the man has to drag a 200-pound dummy and the woman drags a 125-pound dummy. So there is some discrepancies there on, you know, the way that works. Around here any training ... they have to do it exactly. By all means, if they can, you know, do that. And maybe too, a lot of them, like I said, to get the number of points you have to have, like, a trade really helps. So there's probably not many females out there that are plumbers or electricians to start with, eh? So that knocks them down a little bit. But we haven't had – we've had very few apply.

Like Norman, Grant, who earlier noted the presence of a locker-room mentality in the fire station, recognized that women were at a disadvantage, but he stood by the gender-neutral discourse of the level playing field: "To me, whoever earns the job earns the job, okay? That's the way I look at it. No special considerations. Earn the job, it's yours, congratulations. So having said that, it's still – and it's changing, but a lot of it is that male-oriented locker-room kind of atmosphere, right? So that's also a part of it, right? It's not just the pressure of performing and stuff. There's a real lot of locker-room mentality still."

The level playing field is, of course, a myth. In the same way that hiring criteria, such as personality type and fitting in, disadvantage women, the level playing field works to the advantage of men and functions to justify the exclusion of women. Invoking this metaphor is a low-risk discursive strategy for gender inclusion; relatively few women apply for structural firefighting jobs, and those who do may be disqualified for failing the fitness test (witness recent cases in St. John's, Newfoundland, and Chicago, Illinois), not having the right personality, or scoring fewer total points because they lack a trade or sports background. Since most women are at a disadvantage from the start, they must be truly exceptional to make it through the screening process. The trope of the level playing field obscures the gendered practices and structures of inequality that marginalize women in these occupations, while preserving the link between firefighting and masculinity. That said, the recognition that women can be firefighters and perhaps would even be welcomed into the occupation (even if only on a level playing field) does open up a small space for gender integration. It also intimates that there are fissures in the once impermeable boundaries of structural firefighting. In short, differentiation was no longer a tenable solution to the crisis tendency. Firefighters' efforts to distance themselves from hypermasculinity and their talk about including women suggested that they were grappling with a new solution.

Finding a new way to justify patriarchy became especially pressing when firefighters found themselves faced with new and potentially more damaging crises in the wake of the Mountain Park fire. For instance, try as they might, they had been unable to control the flames. The physical devastation was inescapable – widespread and irrevocable damage as far as the eye could see. With their credibility on the line, they had to redeem themselves. How did the firefighters navigate this potential public relations nightmare? How did they frame the losses? And how, in their efforts at damage control, was gender constructed? These are the questions to which I turn in the following chapter.

4 'We Felt Like We Lost': Explaining Failure and Rescuing Masculinity

Firefighters are mandated to protect communities, natural resources, and lives. This imperative is reflected in the mission statement of the forestry administration centre in which the fire occurred: "We will protect life and property and natural resources from catastrophic wildfire impacts" (BC Ministry of Forests, Protection Branch 2004a). This ethic of protection is also evident in job and organizational titles, such as Forest Protection Officer and Protection Branch. Likewise, structural firefighters feel that they have an occupational duty to protect people, homes, and other structures. The first statement on their website reads, "The goal of the Kelowna Fire Department is to provide realistic and effective fire protection and public safety services to all areas of the City of Kelowna" (City of Kelowna 2010).

"We're Out There to Win ..."

Structural and wildland firefighting is also characterized by an ethos of success described as *winning*, which is narrowly defined as "the ability to control or extinguish fire." Many firefighters noted that they were "used to winning" and proudly gave statistics to back up their claims. Bill, an air tanker pilot, recounted the satisfaction associated with catching a fire before it spread: "So, yeah, we're out there to win, to stop the fire. And when a fire is just on the verge and starting to go, and you're working hard and you catch it, everybody feels good."

Notably, winning was, in many cases, described in decidedly masculine terms. Ken, a supervisor in the air tanker program, talked at great length about the organizational culture in his workplace. Ken and I met after a long day of back-to-back interviews at the regional fire centre, so

I was silently relieved that he was so effusive. Without prompting, he described the will to win and the dire consequences of losing (on par with death), using language steeped with aggression and militaristic symbolism:

> Well, we're kinda like – the analogy I would use is we're like emergency surgeons. People don't come to us unless they have a problem. And when we fail, it's a big problem. The patient dies. And that's our reality. So we're all here because we kind of like that ego-stroking, win or lose moment. But when we lose, we beat the shit out of ourselves. We eat our young, quite frankly. We're a brutal organization on ourselves, internally. We take no prisoners. Like our debriefings and our fall meetings are knock down, drag 'em out affairs. But that's because everybody wants to win. And if we can fix something, we'll fix it ... You know, we feel it because we're the last line of defence. We're the best and last hope for that fire a lot of times. And oftentimes, 94 per cent of the time, we win. And so in some years, '97, '98, when we lose, it's a big problem. It starts to cost a million dollars a day and hundreds of people, and homes get threatened, and timber gets lost, and the sky gets all smoky and on and on and on.

Mark, a structural firefighter, used similarly masculinized discourse to describe this ethos of success and, like his colleagues, equated winning with putting out fires: "As a structural firefighter, we're very well trained. We're considered a very aggressive, proactive firefighting group. Something's burning; we go there, we put it out. We don't lose houses; we don't lose foundations. Occasionally it's through the roof, but it gets put out." Hank, a supervisor with thirty years of wildland firefighting experience, remarked that "our people are used to winning," and although on occasion a fire got the best of a crew, more often than not they won: "Most summers, you know, we'd fight fires like we did last summer, but most of the time we'd go out, and maybe the fire kicks our butts one day a week, or something. And then we win six days and we'd feel pretty good about that." Neal, a manager who like Hank had worked his way up through the ranks and had extensive wildland firefighting experience, indicated that his organization was proud of its record of success: "We are a – our organization has been developed over the years where we don't like to lose. We have a couple of, sort of, instilled prides. One is our safety record, and the other one is sort of our success of catching the fires small."

On the flip side, when a fire got away, the mission was deemed a failure. Tellingly, fires that grew larger than four hectares were classified as an "initial attack failure" by wildland firefighters. Chris, a wildland firefighting crew leader, remarked: "We've always been successful, except for these two instances, at keeping the numbers really low. But all of the sudden you start losing over – it's in the hundreds [of homes]. Well, I don't think that's success." For pilots and wildland and structural firefighters, being a "good" firefighter meant not only being an appropriately gendered man but also successfully extinguishing or controlling fires and protecting people and valued resources.

Losing, Credibility, and Gender Crisis

The firefighters could have focused solely on the resources that were saved as a result of their work, but because their occupational cultures were characterized by an ethic of protection and left little room for definitions of success that included the loss of resources, firefighters felt as though they had failed when they were unable to control the Mountain Park fire. Moreover, "losing" this battle took a personal toll on many of the firefighters. Kyle's feelings echoed those of many of his colleagues in the structural fire department: "I remember feeling pretty low on the Saturday morning. Like we just got the shit kicked out of us. You know, we lost like 200-and-some homes, eh? Like in one night. And that sucks. We don't like to lose an outbuilding, let alone a house. And we lost 200 and some? I remember kind of thinking, you know, like what the hell are we doing here? Like we're used to going in there and kickin' ass and getting the job done, you know. And we'd just been hammered, you know." Kyle's colleague, Charlie, explained, somewhat viscerally, that the pain of losing was not only intense (the equivalent of extreme physical pain) but also intensely personal.

> KYLE: Everybody felt bad ... like I had this real bad feeling that we let people down.
> SP: Oh, really?
> KYLE: Yeah, because, I mean, I know everybody felt that way ... Because here we are, we're supposed to be, you know, protecting the city and doing everything we can. The losses were just unbelievable. Like when we heard the numbers, we were just – I mean, you felt like you'd been kicked in the nuts. Like you were just – you felt sick. I really felt sick about it.

Similarly, many wildland firefighters, from supervisors to crew members, took the loss of houses personally. Neal, the manager who remarked that catching fires small was an "instilled pride," stated: "Again, we don't like losing. And to me, I don't know how to say it, it's a personal thing. I'm embarrassed that we lost houses." Josh, an initial attack crew member, agreed: "It does get personal, because a lot – like, guys are really down in the dumps about, like, losing 200-and-some-odd houses." This supervisor tearfully explained that he very much sympathized with other colleagues who had suffered major losses because "you can see how it gets to you ... You can see it's more than a job."

Although many appeared to have come to terms with losing, a sizeable minority were still troubled when I spoke to them a year after the fire. Some were emotional in our interviews, and others explained that it was still difficult to talk about the event. I also heard about numerous others who had not fared well in the aftermath of the fire. For example, firefighters noted that some of their colleagues had left their jobs (that is, taken early retirement or gone on to other jobs), were on stress leave, or were having marital difficulties that they attributed to the fire.

Firefighters may have been used to winning, but in the case of the Mountain Park fire, they clearly felt like they had lost. However, it was not simply because they were accustomed to winning that they were so upset about the losses. The firefighters were acutely aware that the public was concerned about the scope of the fire damage. This meant that their competence and credibility as good firefighters could be called into question. Credibility – being worthy of confidence – is a socially conferred status. An audience is required to grant credibility, like heroism (Lois 2003) and masculinity (Kimmel 1994); one cannot bestow it upon oneself.

If the public turned against the firefighters, they had much to lose. The lawsuit being faced by the City of Kelowna firefighters made the credibility issue especially pressing because they could be held liable for the losses in the event of an unfavourable verdict. However, the structural firefighters could also rely, to some extent, on their greater social and cultural capital (Bourdieu 1986) to weather the storm. As one supervisor observed, "we're largely appreciated in the community." Wildland firefighters, on the other hand, were dealing with a more chronic public relations problem.

Prior to the fire the firefighters working for the Ministry of Forests had been contending with credibility concerns unlike those of the structural

Figure 4.1 Charred remains (photograph by Cory Bialecki)

firefighters. There had been a history of conflict between the Ministry of Forests and the public over prescribed burns and air quality issues that had given the organization a bad name in some camps. In addition, wildland firefighters and pilots had the dubious distinction of having fought on other large interface fires in which homes had been lost.

Structural firefighters from the City of Kelowna had never lost houses to an interface fire prior to the summer of 2003. Furthermore, wildland firefighters, as employees of the provincial government, were subject to stereotypes that characterized government workers as underworked, overpaid, and inefficient. The Ministry of Forests was painfully aware of this perception, as evidenced in some of the rules of decorum for its employees. For example, wildland firefighters were instructed not to sit down to eat lunch while working on interface fires, out of concern that the public would make negative assumptions about their work ethic. Similarly, although wildland firefighters routinely used humour to ease tension and reduce stress, they had to be mindful of their surroundings when doing so because their antics could give the impression that they did not take the fire seriously. Wildland firefighters and their supervisors had to be very careful of the manner in which they comported themselves because they were always under public scrutiny. Pilots were also employed by the provincial government and by association were subjected to some of the same surveillance as were wildland firefighters. However, they were also protected by the occupational prestige of their profession.

Despite these differences in capital between firefighting groups, all had a stake in reclaiming their image as competent (gender-coded as masculine) firefighters because their patriarchal privilege depended on it. When these exemplars of firefighting masculinity could not control the advancing flames, and millions of dollars of property and resources were destroyed (that is, when the firefighters "lost"), a crisis tendency (Connell 1995) in the gender regime of firefighting was born. Losing created a threat to the firefighters' credibility as competent and appropriately gendered firefighters, because in the firefighting world gender is constructed using binary logic. Good firefighters are masculine, and bad firefighters are unmasculine or feminine. Femininity is equated with poor firefighting skills; therefore, losing was itself potential evidence of a collective failure of firefighting masculinity.[1] It became possible, then, that this configuration of masculinity was not necessary for success (that is, to win).

If firefighters could not effectively thwart a full-blown credibility crisis, their claim that successful firefighters must embody firefighting masculinity would certainly ring hollow. The illogicality of their collective story would be revealed, and the edifice upon which their claims to difference, superiority, and patriarchal privilege were built would be severely compromised. In short, their solution to patriarchy would no longer be tenable. In such a case, firefighting masculinity could not be invoked as readily to justify the exclusion of women and Other men. Firefighting masculinity, like hegemonic masculinity, confers significant privileges or patriarchal dividends (Connell 1995) on those who are thought to embody it. One of those dividends is the control over relatively lucrative working-class occupations (Paap 2006); in firefighting there is a gendered division of labour in which men hold the best jobs and the resources and power to keep it that way. Losing the battle against the fire was especially troublesome because it had the potential to undercut the masculine privileges enjoyed by the firefighters. In short, when the firefighters lost the battle against the fire, they had to win the battle over the legitimacy of patriarchy.

So did the firefighters' resolution to the crisis tendency (specifically, the ways in which they accomplished gender) further entrench gender inequality or did it open up possibilities for change? In the case of the former, what strategies did firefighters use to reclaim firefighting masculinity? Or, in the case of the latter, what were the mechanisms of gender disruption? These are the questions to which I turn my attention in the following sections.

Shifting Responsibility and Saving Face

One structural firefighting administrator insightfully noted that the collective masculinity of the firefighters under his supervision was troubled by the events of Black Friday: "Part of the mentality is that we can pretty much do anything, you know, and that goes back to the macho image. And that got bashed that day; that got bashed really hard that day." For the most part, though, firefighters did not make connections between losing and the implications for masculine privilege. Rather, they went to great lengths to justify their loss, drawing on the following explanations: (i) there was really "nothing you could do"; (ii) they had to follow safety precautions; or (iii) other firefighters failed to do their job properly. Some also deflected attention away from losing by minimizing the losses and focusing on the positive outcomes. This talk, I argue, worked to defuse the tensions in gender relations that were generated by losing.

Common to firefighters from all groups was the narrative that shifted some of the responsibility for the losses incurred to other groups or to forces beyond their control. Finger pointing was a common means for firefighters to transfer accountability, and this was most evident when they blamed others for the losses by insinuating or claiming outright that the others were inept.

In this blame game the firefighters attempted to set up their colleagues from other groups as incompetent Others. Rick, a structural firefighter, maintained that while it was "easy to talk ... somebody has to pay." Soon afterwards, he claimed that interface fires in which structures were lost were "screw ups" by the Ministry of Forests and that the Mountain Park fire was no exception. Moreover, he hoped that wildland firefighters had learned something from structural firefighters about how to fight fires, presumably so that these "screw ups" could be prevented in the future:

> Whenever you talk to a forester, a forest fire fighter, they call it "contained." And you know ... what the hell is this contained? 'Cause we don't contain; we fight. We fight fires. That's what we are; we're fire fighters, not fire containers, you know. And they learned that from us this year ... They don't have the ability to move water. Like our trucks can pump thousands and thousands of gallons of water a minute. And we can move it miles. We can pump from one truck to the other and move thousands of gallons of water. The forestry run around with little things on their back, and shovels and hose. So they dig a big circle around a fire and let it burn itself out. They sort of learned, well, these assholes have the ability to go in and fight the fire. And whether they learn it and use it, I don't know.

A number of Rick's colleagues blamed wildland firefighters for "letting" the fire get to the city limits, lamenting the fact that because it was so immense by the time it got to them, there was little they could do to stop it. One supervisor, after noting that structural firefighters could not stop the fire, went on to point out that wildland firefighters ran, implying that they were not much help: "We thought we could stop it. We thought, 'Put a lot of guys at it, a lot of water on a big fire, you should be able to put it out' ... The forestry guys said, 'Look, there [is] no fire truck made big enough to put that fire out.' The helicopters, no. You gotta realize forestry had a couple hundred guys out there too. There was probably five or so hundred guys out there that night. Some of them running for the water, you know."

Wildland firefighters were aware that some of the blame was placed on them and in like fashion did some finger pointing of their own. Several wildland firefighters indicated that the Kelowna Fire Department was non-compliant when it came to implementing fire prevention practices. For example, Sam directed at least some of the blame towards the fire chief for neglecting to take the prevention measures that the Ministry of Forests had recommended almost a decade earlier:

SAM: [The structural fire chief] is not the guy that we can hang this all on. There's no way. I mean, he's just one component of it. And he's one component that's massive in media. But he's pulled the wool over a lot of people's eyes. In the community, in the public.

SP: In terms of what went on or in terms of ...

SAM: Oh well, our organization has been to that community many times. You look around at all of our large centres ... most places we have great working relationships with the fire department. You have to, right? We're all in the same business. And a lot of times our wildfires threaten their structure fires or potential structure fires. So we go to these communities, we go to these fire departments, we go to these cities, we go to these fire chiefs, and say, "You guys have a problem here." And the normal response is, "Yeah, we know that. And how can we work together to fix it?" Our guys, our people, our folks went to Kelowna in 1994 and 1996 ... Simulated fire: you're going to have a fire come to you in this direction; you'll lose 40 homes, in simulation, under these conditions. [The structural fire chief] was there and said, "That'll never happen."

More often, wildland firefighters were veiled in their critique. They had been instructed by administrators not to make disparaging comments about the Kelowna Fire Department because the structural firefighters did not want to be held liable for the losses. According to one wildland supervisor, "I've had many phone calls from the chief there, saying, 'You're putting us – you're saying things that weren't true, your staff are, and it makes us look like we're liable.'" As a result, many comments regarding structural firefighters were prefaced by statements like "not to take anything away from the structural side" or "not a criticism towards them." It appeared that wildland firefighters wanted to say more, but the organizationally imposed gag order prevented it. Instead, they implied incompetence. For instance, one wildland firefighter, Kathy, explained that on Black Friday she had not felt they were in danger (they were "ready to do structural protection or maybe a burn off") but that the structural firefighters were not comfortable staying (they "removed themselves"); therefore, the wildland firefighters were given the word to leave, which was "difficult" for them.

Wildland firefighters and pilots were just as likely to point fingers at the public, corporations, and other government agencies, especially for a lack of fire prevention practices. This was a particularly contentious issue because wildland firefighters and pilots felt they were blamed for losses that they had in fact tried to prevent. The irony of this situation was not lost on one supervisor:

> You know, I spent ten years, before I got this job – my big role was the wildland urban interface ... I was trying to convince city councils, municipalities, ... the premier's office that we need restrictive covenance on subdivisions to prevent them from putting shake roofs. To have setbacks, to have fuel modification programs, to have, to have, to have, to have. The opening line of my speech was, "It's not a question of *if*, but a matter of *when*, we're gonna have home losses on a parallel with Oakland," which was the fire in 1991 that burnt up 3,000 homes – or 1,000 homes in Oakland. And lo and behold, it happened. And I found that frustrating, and that pissed me off because that was like a foregone conclusion from the early to mid eighties, that we were going down this road ... And we'd talk to the insurance companies, we'd talk to everybody that would listen. Not just media, whole organizations. And then we have a fire and it's our fault! [laughter] You know, Mother Nature starts it, we don't catch it, it must be – someone must have fucked up.

"There's Nothing You Can Do"

Firefighters also justified losing by transferring at least some of the responsibility for the losses to forces beyond their control, often making explicit reference to Mother Nature. When I mentioned to Trevor, a structural firefighter, that some of his colleagues felt responsible for the losses, he replied: "I think a lot of us did [feel guilty] afterwards ... And thinking that you could have done more, you know, after the fact. Although when you analyse it and sit down and talk to the guys, there's really nothing else you could have done. It was beyond anything we could have controlled, you know, so. And that was tough, that was tough to accept." In a similar vein, Trevor's colleague Ben remarked, "We weren't used to having ... such a magnitude coming at us that there's nothing that we could have done to stop that part of it. It was a monster."

Firefighters from other groups used similar discursive tactics. For example, a pilot explained that the heavy losses of the 2003 fire season had been due, in part, to the uncontrollable force of Mother Nature: "You realize early on that Mother Nature, when it decides it's gonna burn, it's gonna burn, no matter what man's gonna do, and that's what happened last summer." His colleague, a unit crew supervisor, felt a similar sense of futility: "Nature's gonna go where she wants to go. She'll pretty much do what she's gonna do." Mother Nature was also invoked in reference to extinguishing the fire, as one structural firefighter noted: "Mother Nature started the fire, let it burn for like 25 days, and Mother Nature basically put it out, with rain. And that was the only thing that could do it."

That the fire was unstoppable was a position that some firefighters were willing to take. The "home run fire" provided a discursive escape hatch, a way to explain losing the battle against the fire. However, this manoeuvre was not without its dangers, because firefighters' livelihoods (and cultural capital) depend on their ability to control or extinguish fire. However, it was less risky than the alternative: foregoing the masculine privileges that depend on the successful defence of patriarchy.

Safety First

Wildland firefighters and pilots also explained the losses by pointing to organizational safety imperatives that mandated and curtailed the scope of their efforts. When asked to give a chronology of the fire's progression, a supervisor in the air tanker program relayed the following: "The lightning strike hit sometime at two in the morning, or something like that, and it was already going nuts when they spotted it. So they put a tanker request in at five in the morning. Well, we're bound by Canadian aviation regulations and fire reality that if we started flying at five in the morning, those airplanes are done at five at night. Twelve hour-days ... and that's a safety thing, and I agree with it. So we didn't launch until about eight in the morning, which gave us until eight at night, which is fine."

Safety was also invoked to ease the frustration of losing. As Lionel explained, "When we start losing on a grander scale, it is tough, it's really frustrating, but the most important thing for us is staying alive." While it was frustrating to lose, this supervisor (and many of the firefighters working under him) made it known that safety trumped winning at any cost: "We don't burn people for trees. Well, that's a pretty harsh statement. What we're saying is we don't put people in jeopardy for any resource or any value. Public safety, our crew safety, is paramount."

Minimizing Losses

Firefighters, primarily wildland firefighters and pilots, diminished the importance or value of the resources that were destroyed by the fire. They made numerous remarks like "they're just homes," "they can replace most of their possessions," and "in the long run they'll be further ahead financially." Sherry, who revealed earlier in the interview that "you feel kind of crappy" when houses burn, agreed that it was difficult to lose houses, but she immediately followed with, "But even then, it's just a house. It's just a house. You may not have got your pictures out, but guess what, your family has doubles." However, she soon countered with, "But then again your whole family's houses might have been burned," suggesting that this strategy did not entirely ameliorate her sense of loss. One firefighter even went so far as to say that houses are "just another fuel type." He went on to transfer the blame to homeowners: "Houses burn, yes, they do. We didn't build them there; somebody else did. We didn't make them combustible. They chose not to clean out their back yard." Comments such as these were rooted in firefighters' irritation with public apathy and the accompanying lack of fire prevention measures, but they also provided a way of smoothing over the tensions that were generated by the loss of valued resources.

"It Wasn't All Bad"

Finally, firefighters from all groups transferred attention from losses to more positive fire outcomes. For example, a number of structural firefighters and administrators felt that the fire was a "proving ground," one in which their skills and experience were put to the test and they came out standing. This was especially true for recent hires or those who had transferred to new positions. Eight new firefighters were hired by the Kelowna Fire Department in 2003, and they had been on the job for just ten days before they were called into duty for the Mountain Park fire. Mike felt that the "initiation by fire" was beneficial because it allowed him to gain the trust and respect of his colleagues.

Firefighters from all groups suggested that things could have been worse, by pointing to the fact that there had been few serious injuries and no lost lives. The pilots who had lost three of their comrades that summer were the exception in this case. Trevor, who had noted earlier that he and his colleagues had felt guilty about losing houses, pointed out that while the devastation caused by the fire was great, fortunately there were no deaths among structural firefighters: "Not much left of the houses actually. I've never seen a house burn down so hot ... even the cement foundation, it overheated and it actually turned into almost like a dust ... It was that hot. I mean there was nothing left ... The biggest thing is it's a miracle that nobody got hurt, and nobody died." This theme was echoed by a wildland supervisor who emphasized that despite the difficult circumstances, his employees sustained very few injuries: "Through the whole thing last year, another part of my job was making sure that everybody was still focused in on that [safety] side of our business. Yes, it's serious, yeah, we've lost a sawmill, yeah, we've lost a bunch of houses, unfortunately we lost some pilots. We worked probably three or four million man hours last year, and we had hardly any major injuries at all."

A few firefighters also directed attention to the resources that were saved because of their efforts. Even Charlie, the structural firefighter who had said earlier that losing was like getting "kicked in the nuts," managed to put a positive spin on things: "It took probably a week to put it into perspective and realize that, you know, yeah okay, we lost all those, but if we hadn't been there, it would have been like 2,000 houses would have been burnt. That whole hillside would have been burnt." One supervisor in the Kelowna Fire Department stressed that they worked hard to turn a negative into a positive by encouraging firefighters to focus on successes. This strategy did not work for everybody, however. Mark explained: "Everybody goes, 'Oh don't think about the 200 and [pauses] I try to forget about that, the 200-and-some-odd houses that were lost. Think of the thousands of houses you saved.' Well yeah, whatever. That's not the point. The point is we lost houses, and we don't lose houses." Several wildland firefighters highlighted their success at preventing losses. Tom underscored the "saves" that his group made: "You know, there was a lot of fires ... that we did catch that had a lot of potential to be just as catastrophic." However, he and his colleagues bemoaned the fact that while they had some major successes, the public never heard about them.

Notably, both of the women wildland firefighters who worked on the front lines of the fire were, like their male colleagues, keen to explain the losses. Perhaps this is not surprising, since they were insiders and, as such, derived some benefits from holding a masculine-coded job (such as relatively high pay). Privileged women have an interest in resisting reforms that could undermine their status (Connell 2009). However, while these women had some motivation for upholding patriarchy, they faced a number of disadvantages simply because they were women. I discuss these in detail in chapter 6. In many ways, they were caught in a double bind. If they focused on explaining the losses, they could exonerate themselves (and their colleagues) and avoid a full-fledged credibility crisis. Yet, this would also mean that the system that marginalized them as women would likely remain intact.

The Costs of Losing

Clearly, losing did not bode well for the firefighters. They viewed the fire as a loss, a loss that they took very personally. One could conclude that losing resulted in "spoiled" identities (Goffman 1963, 19) and, therefore, firefighters were attempting to resist stigmatization; their character was blemished and, therefore, "discreditable" (4). Following this line of reasoning, firefighters engaged in identity work in an attempt to vindicate themselves by drawing on various justifications for losing. An important piece of this Goffmanian puzzle is missing, however, and that piece has to do with masculinities in crisis. The firefighters were attempting to signify to themselves and others that they were competent firefighters and masculine men. Goffman's formulation of impression management and, later, theories of identity work (for example see Snow and Anderson 1987; Snow and Anderson 1994) do not theorize gender and gendered power. As a result, they cannot explain why winning was so important to firefighters (other than to point to stigma avoidance) or how the firefighters' justifications for losing were linked to a broader political agenda of keeping Others out and protecting patriarchal privilege.

Hegemonic patterns of gender practice are only effective to the extent that they explain patriarchy, in other words to the extent that they are generally believed to provide an answer to the problem of inequality between women and men (Connell 1995). For many years the answer in wildland and structural firefighting was based on the claim that particular gendered characteristics were required to be an effective firefighter, the implication being that only certain men embodied the pattern of gender required for success. As long as firefighters continued to win on the firefighting front, their justifications for excluding Others went largely unchallenged.

However, when the firefighters could not bring the fire under control, two crises ensued: a natural disaster of unprecedented proportions and a crisis in gender relations. There were, then, two battles fought in the Mountain Park fire, one against the forces of Mother Nature and one against a sea change in gender relations in the world of work.

There was much at stake in these parallel battles. Most obviously, millions of dollars of property and resources were at risk of being consumed by the flames. In the end, those resources were reduced to thousands of hectares of incinerated rubble. But this disaster was not solely about economic losses. The devastation also precipitated a crisis of equal significance in the gender regimes of local firefighting organizations. The given answer to gender inequality no longer made sense in the wake of the fire. Even hand-picked exemplars of firefighting masculinity could not stop the flames. As a result, the firefighters' claims to masculine superiority, and the mechanism for exclusion upon which those claims rested, were further compromised.

When the firefighters could not control the fire, the boundaries between insiders and outsiders became tenuous and potentially permeable. This opened up the possibility that the previously spurned and excluded Others were eligible for group membership. If current group members did not possess the requisite qualifications or those qualifications were not, in fact, required for successful firefighting, it would become less certain that the characteristics in question were actually necessary for group participation. Therefore, Others (who ostensibly did not posses these traits) could do the job just as well and would be newly eligible for membership.

In the aftermath of the fire the once impregnable firefighting fortress was no longer impervious to the social forces of gender equality. Firefighters had to successfully address this crisis tendency in order to maintain their power to keep Others out – a predicament that generated a great deal of defensive posturing. Firefighters focused on explaining why they had lost and attempted to signify to themselves and others (for example, the media, the public, and the author) that, despite the devastation, they remained competent, masculine firefighters. Their credibility and the patriarchal privileges that went along with it depended on the effectiveness of this damage control campaign.

Somewhat ironically, the firefighters' focus on winning and their narrow definition of success set them up to "fail." Wildfires burn hotter and longer today than they did in previous decades (Desmond 2007), and climate change promises more fire ignitions, larger fires, and longer fire seasons (Flannigan et al. 2006; Gillett et al. 2004). The risk of home run fires is extremely high in this era of public resistance to prescribed burn programs, homeowner apathy to wildfire prevention measures, heightened concerns about air quality, pine beetle infestations, and a lack of government funding for ground fuel removal (CBC News 2009a, 2009b, 2010). Controlling or extinguishing interface fires is increasingly difficult in this context, yet it is precisely these criteria that define success for wildland and structural firefighters.

If firefighters continue to define success so narrowly, they will also continue to "lose" battles against home run fires. Thus, the threat of a credibility crisis, and a concomitant loss of patriarchal privilege and resources, will always loom large. Firefighting masculinities will most likely remain in a perpetual state of crisis, feeding firefighters' defensiveness and intensifying their efforts to maintain their position by excluding Others from their ranks.

There were additional costs that resulted from the firefighters' efforts to defend themselves. In their attempts to provide plausible explanations for the losses, the firefighters engaged in a great deal of finger pointing. So, in the very act of attempting to solidify their status as competent firefighters, they created and fortified boundaries between firefighting groups that foreclosed the possibility of the occupational alliances that could have come about as a result of the fire. This raises questions about the firefighters' ability to work together in the future, not only in undertaking fire prevention measures but also in battling another interface fire.[2]

These boundaries also reinforced an occupational hierarchy among firefighting groups. As I noted earlier, non-structural firefighters did not go into the fire with the same degree of capital as did their structural colleagues. In theory, the fire could have provided an opportunity for non-structural firefighters to increase their status, but this was not the case. Instead, the Mountain Park fire strengthened the hierarchy among firefighting groups: structural firefighters became heroes, while others who toiled just as strenuously did not. In the next chapter I explain how the hierarchy came about, how firefighters responded to this crisis tendency, and the consequences for gender relations both between and within firefighting groups.

5 Navigating Hierarchy and Contesting Masculinities

And shouts ring out for those who dare
To face such hell of smoke and glare, –
The gallant Fire-Brigade
(unidentified source cited in Cooper 1995)

Structural firefighters have long been admired by the general public, a phenomenon that did not appear to wane after the Mountain Park fire. Wildland firefighters, by comparison, were keenly aware that they did not garner the same respect, praise, and resources as did the structural firefighters, despite their extensive efforts to contain the fire. This generated a great deal of intergroup tension and animosity, which continued to smoulder nearly a year after the last flames had been extinguished. I heard numerous disparaging comments (largely unsolicited) that were often, although not exclusively, directed at the City of Kelowna firefighters, especially the fire chief, who was a favourite target. Many wildland firefighters were frustrated over what they felt was unfair recognition of the City's firefighters and a lack of praise for forestry firefighters and equipment operators, who were "really" the ones who took on the most important and dangerous firefighting tasks.

Greg, a long-time veteran of the forest service and a supervisor during the fire, was one of the first firefighters whom I interviewed. Diplomatic, measured, and thoughtful, his stories revealed the first signs of the depth and character of the tensions between firefighting groups. Brought to tears in relaying the tenacity, dedication, and hard work of his colleagues, Greg felt strongly that their efforts should have been better recognized and not overshadowed by those of structural firefighters:

> I think the role, and what was accomplished by our people on the ground, doesn't get the attention that it deserves. And I think that has a real psychological impact on our firefighters and our equipment operators. I think that the glory all goes to the [structural] fire departments ... Our staff, our crews, the forest service crews, were the last people out, after the fire department had left. Our guys were the ones who held and maintained that fireguard on the south side. It wasn't the fire department who did that. It was our staff that did that, our firefighter personnel who held the line. It was our staff who risked themselves in injury, in maintaining that line. It was our front line folks and equipment operators that put in that [fire] guard, that worked through the heat and the dust, and the hot and the dry. It's our people who do all of that. Those equipment operators chug away, day and night sometimes, twenty-four hours a day, and they get very little recognition. The glory all goes to the [City of Kelowna] fire department. And that in itself has a huge impact to the morale. And somehow the credit has to go where it rightfully belongs.

Greg's sentiments were echoed time and again by his colleagues in later interviews.

This social hierarchy between firefighting groups made problematic the ongoing accomplishment of firefighting masculinity. Wildland firefighters worked long and hard to contain the fire and, in the end, they lost the battle. As competent firefighters are masculine firefighters, the losses threatened the long-established link between firefighting and masculinity. To make matters worse, wildland firefighters received very little recognition for their efforts, while their counterparts were showered with praise and rewards.

Structural firefighters faced a somewhat different dilemma. Like wildland firefighters, they felt they had lost the battle against the fire, but they were held up as heroes by the media and the public. Not only did they have to prove that they were deserving of the accolades, but masculinity dynamics compelled them to maintain their positioning at the top of the hierarchy, a point to which I return below.

Firefighters responded to this crisis tendency by using discursive strategies that worked to undermine the occupational and gender credibility of firefighters from other groups. In so doing, they drew on prevailing constructions of hegemonic masculinity that simultaneously positioned some firefighters as superior (ultimately as more "masculine") and others as subordinate. Somewhat ironically, structural firefighters – the very group that was unable to protect the most valued resource (homes) – were more successful at this than were other groups. They cemented their status as heroes and continued to reap the benefits more than a year after the fire.

These social dynamics raise a number of questions. Why were structural firefighters able to escape criticism for the loss of over two hundred and fifty homes? Why did they receive so much more prestige and status than did the other firefighters, when it was clear that all the groups played an important role in extinguishing the fire? Why were some firefighters able to stake a successful claim to exemplary masculinity, and what were the conditions that enabled them to do so? And, finally, did these struggles over masculinity disrupt the doing of gender?

First, a point of clarification is in order. Long before the fire began, there were occupational boundaries between firefighting groups, and status differences between wildland and structural firefighters. For example, a high-ranking administrator in the forestry department mentioned that in years past some structural fire departments had been reluctant to receive forest-fire training from wildland firefighters because the latter were "seasonal" workers and viewed as less professional. The hierarchy between groups, then, was not created by the events surrounding the fire but was further exacerbated by them.

There are a number of common-sense ways to explain why structural firefighters received more recognition, prestige, and status during the fire and in the months that followed. Structural firefighters were the last line of defence for the city of Kelowna; people turned to them in their time of need. In addition, since the events of 11 September 2001, structural firefighters have been portrayed as heroes, especially in the media. Combined with the fact that wildland firefighters had ongoing public relations issues, this meant that going into the fire the structural firefighters had more social and cultural capital.

While each of these factors helps to explain the structural firefighters' coming out on top, there were also some less obvious, but theoretically significant, social dynamics that played a role. These dynamics necessitate a look beyond micro-level social interactions to the broader institutional structures and culture in which they were embedded (Fuchs Epstein 1992). In the case of the Mountain Park fire, the organization of the firefighting efforts and the media representations of firefighters had important implications for the power struggles between firefighting groups and for the ability of structural firefighters to prevail.

The ways in which the fire attack was orchestrated meant that structural firefighters and non-structural firefighters inhabited different physical and geographical spaces. This was significant for the level of support received by each group. During the fire several staging areas were set up where firefighting crews were organized and given instructions before they headed out to the fire zone. The staging areas for the heavy equipment operators and the wildland firefighters were on the outskirts of the city because these sites were in close proximity to the areas in which the wildland firefighting crews were working (usually deep in the forest, especially at the beginning of the fire). The wildland firefighters' command post was set up at the Okanagan Mountain Park headquarters, located in a small town about fifty kilometres south of Kelowna. Pilots were dispatched from regional airport bases that were even further afield.

In contrast, structural firefighters were located at the main fire station, right in the heart of Kelowna. The emergency operations centre was situated in the same building and housed many administrative personnel who were part of the firefighting efforts; as a result, it attracted a large number of reporters. The geographical location of the main fire station and the fact that structural firefighters fought the fire within the city limits meant that both on and off duty they were much more accessible to reporters.

These institutional arrangements facilitated relationships with the media that resulted in more coverage for structural firefighters. As Greg noted, "the people that [the media] interview, because they're readily available, are the people in the fire department, in the halls." Many other non-structural firefighters also pointed out that because structural firefighters were accessible to the media, they received a great deal of coverage. For example, Bob, a thirty-year veteran with the forestry service, stated: "You know, [the media] could go to the number one fire hall, and they could corner some fireman and they could see the trucks and all of that. You know, we tried to make the fire line available to media people, but it was all, you know, you gotta watch for safety there too, right? So we had escorted tours at different times, and different times we'd take them up and let them take some pictures from the air or whatever ... I mean, it wasn't as open as the fire hall was, sort of thing." Bob notes that safety concerns were another obstacle to gaining access to wildland firefighters. If reporters wanted to interview wildland firefighters, they had to go to the staging area, which was out of town, or to the fire zone, which was not always feasible owing to safety issues.

As the main fire station was more accessible to the public, most of the donations to the firefighting efforts arrived there. Structural firefighters received everything from truckloads of food to crates of cold beer. Volunteers were also on hand to provide complimentary massages, make sandwiches, and provide moral support. Meanwhile most of the wildland firefighters and pilots were stationed in base camps far from the centre of the city.

Lionel, an air attack officer who supervised pilots during the fire, revealed that he and his crew members resented the structural firefighters because of the special treatment that they received: "And I know that there was lots of, you know, 'Well, those poor [structural] fire guys.' They're kind of, oh yeah, poor babies, you know. They're getting back rubs, they're getting beers. We can't have any beers on base. You know, we don't get any of that stuff. And there's no recognition. So a certain amount of, what do you call it, dissension? Oh yeah, the poor structural guys." The general sentiment of the non-structural firefighters was that structural firefighters received preferential treatment. The organizational arrangements of the firefighting efforts were directly related not only to the amount of resources and support available (or not available) to the different groups of firefighters but also to the amount of media exposure that each group received.

The Making of Heroes

The organization of labour during the fire gave the media and the public greater access to structural firefighters, which resulted in more media coverage. Based on newspaper accounts, structural firefighters (especially the fire chief) received considerably more print media coverage than did any other groups or individuals involved in the firefighting efforts. Technical fire information was obtained both from forest service information officers and the chief of the Kelowna Fire Department; however, the majority of firefighter personal interest stories were about structural firefighters, especially the Kelowna fire chief. While there were several articles about firefighters from other groups, for the most part they appeared near the end of the fire. For example, more than two weeks after the fire had started, one headline in the *Kelowna Daily*

Courier exclaimed: "Unsung heroes: Heavy equipment operators have put their lives on the line fighting the Okanagan Mountain blaze, but respect has been hard to find" (Poulsen 2003). Even the army, brought in to provide support services to the front-line firefighters (such as putting out hot spots and performing mop-up duties), received a relatively large share of media coverage.

Chris, a wildland firefighter crew leader, noted that, as a result of the unequal coverage, the public gave more credit to the structural firefighters than to the wildland firefighters. He also commented that owing to these events, the forestry service eventually hired more media relations people: "And [the presence of additional media relations people] I think came directly out of Kelowna, for the most part. Because of the war between the structural and the forestry. Because of the huge battle, and we saw who won in the hearts of the people because there was the media again … It was all the media on them, and then none of the media on [us], so if you only hear one side of the story, you're going to vote what?" According to Chris, not only did structural firefighters fare better than did wildland firefighters in terms of media coverage, but they also won another important battle – the recognition, support, and adoration of the public. Chris was not alone in his sentiments; numerous other wildland firefighters were critical of the coverage provided by the media.

Conversely, a number of structural firefighters complained that they had received, and continued to receive, more attention than they desired. Several mentioned that they were "hounded" by reporters, and one veteran called the event "the fire that never goes away" in reference to the donations that continued to arrive at the fire station and the praise that was still directed their way even one year later. Another explained that while he appreciated the public support, it was also overwhelming: "After a while you just, you know, you feel like if one more stranger comes up and hugs me, I'm gonna drop kick 'em."

The Media as Reputational Entrepreneurs: "Thanks for Being Our Heroes!"

During the fire and in the weeks that followed, the print media covered numerous stories about firefighters. Both of the local newspapers drew on dominant cultural discourses and symbols of heroism in these stories. Many framed firefighters as heroes, either explicitly (through the use of the word *hero*) or implicitly (by referring to firefighters as "courageous" and "selfless," for example). In addition, the *Daily Courier* printed pull-out posters that read "Thanks for Being Our Heroes!" and urged readers to "show your gratitude and display this poster in your window." The media have been involved in the business of hero making for more than two centuries (Houchin Winfield 2003), and this event was no exception.

Again, many of these stories involved the Kelowna fire chief and, to a lesser degree, the structural firefighters who worked under him. Given the valorization of structural firefighters since the events of 11 September 2001 (Langewiesche 2002; Lorber 2002), which had occurred only two years prior to the fire, it was clearly strategic for the media to portray structural firefighters as heroic. The media's objective is to create and retain reader interest (Altheide 2001), and one way to accomplish this is to design human interest stories that attract readers and maintain their loyalty. Successful stories create "collective attention" and encourage "shared identification" among audience members, and this is only possible to the extent that readers identify with the principal characters and settings (Fine and White 2002, 57). Consequently, the media favoured the structural fire department because they likely recognized that their audience would identify more readily with structural firefighters as heroes. In an effort to promote readers' direct identification with characters, the media essentially acted as "reputational entrepreneurs"; that is, they shaped the reputations of structural firefighters in ways that benefited media interests (Fine 1996, 1162). Wildland firefighters – a more diverse group with more women and First Nations firefighters – did not fit so neatly into the heroism frame.

The ways in which the media frame events also has implications for the social construction of gender, especially in the aftermath of tragedy or disaster (Drew 2004; Grewal 2003; Projansky 1998). Media representations enforce and reproduce culturally dominant gender norms, symbols, ideologies, and stereotypes (Connell 2000a; Dworkin and Wachs 2000; Howard and Prividera 2004; Scanlon 1999), and because the use of conventional categories and familiar roles conveys stability, this may be especially true in times of crisis (Cox, Long, Jones, and Handler 2008; Lorber 2002). Media also have a vested interest in supporting culturally dominant conceptions of manliness because they want readers to connect with the characters in their stories. Perhaps not surprisingly then, hegemonic configurations of masculinity were embedded in the heroism rhetoric and championed by the media, especially for structural firefighters.

Two days after Black Friday, one headline declared, "Hard fought battle: For every home lost, firefighters saved two, says weary fire chief" (Plant 2003). The body of the article was punctuated by references to the dangers in which firefighters placed themselves, including the injuries sustained (for example, "the fire prompted fierce firefighting that could have turned deadly"). It also relayed an incident in which firefighters were "trapped" by the flames; however, the reporter was quick to note that "once [the] flames died down, the men fought their way back in and put out spot fires." Several days later *Capital News*, reporting on the story of the trapped firefighters, printed the following headline: "Training and experience kept trapped firefighters calm" (Waters 2003). Another headline in the *Daily Courier* exclaimed: "Hot stuff: Studly forest fire point men are not just a couple of hosers" (Seymour 2003). These are only several examples of many in which the media implicitly referenced culturally dominant ideals of masculinity such as strength, aggression, courage in the face of danger, heterosexuality, and stoicism. As in other tragedies, the media used this event to protect and articulate dominant gender narratives (Projansky 1998). Further, they evoked and perpetuated the parameters of manhood, which ultimately provided a context of support for the dynamic reproduction of a heroic firefighting masculinity.

On the whole, the public appeared to embrace the new heroes. They enthusiastically participated in a yellow-ribbon campaign, posted signs of gratitude around the city, attended public events to honour firefighters, supported a number of fund-raising causes, and donated a generous amount of time and money to the firefighting efforts. Wildland firefighters, however, expressed mixed emotions about the hero atmosphere that permeated the community because they did not feel that the praise was necessarily directed at them (despite the fact that there were some signs and media stories that focused on non-structural firefighters). When asked how he felt about seeing the signs, Josh, a wildland firefighter in his third season as a crew member, remarked:

Um, yeah, we saw [the signs] every time we drove in. And, like here at the [forestry] base, there's somewhat – there's some animosity between us and the KFD, the Kelowna Fire Department ... Like because they stopped the fire when it was all in the houses, they kind of got the glory. And it's like we all know, we couldn't do anything when it's in that kind of [forest conditions] ... So it was kind of like, well, we did all this work and, despite our efforts, this is going to happen and you can't stop it. You know, we had posters and stuff, but as it started kind of slowing down, we were kind of, you know, we were back to doing our job, and those guys are still kind of in the glory.

So, according to Josh, not only did the structural firefighters receive more credit because they were battling house fires, but they stayed in the limelight when the wildland firefighters went off to fight forest fires in other areas. As Josh and his colleagues were largely overlooked in the media coverage of the fire, they were somewhat sceptical about the heroism messages that permeated the local media. It is also likely that the placement of the signs signalled that they were directed at structural firefighters. One wildland firefighting supervisor noted that signs were erected in front of the fire stations of structural firefighters and in other locations where they could be expected to see them. Overall, the imputation of heroic efforts did not seem to resonate with wildland firefighters (men or women). This is understandable given their credibility crisis and relative lack of social and cultural capital in the aftermath of the fire.

In contrast, most of the structural firefighters recognized that the heroism discourse was directed at them. One rookie firefighter, Jeff, maintained that being called a hero was a great "morale booster"; however, he noted, "I don't think there's anyone who wants to be called a hero or anything; like it's just, you know, that's what we're paid to do." All of the structural firefighters denied being heroes and gave the trite answer that what they did was just "part of the job."

Performing a risky or gallant act alone does not qualify one as a hero. Heroism is a socially conferred status; to be regarded as a hero one must be recognized and labelled as such by others (Lois 2003). This social convention may have precluded structural firefighters from identifying themselves as heroes, but their stories often revealed an implicit perception that they performed courageous, if not heroic, acts in their everyday work. While the structural firefighters claimed to reject the hero label, a hero-like narrative was woven into their talk. Following are statements from three veteran firefighters who denied being heroes:

If somebody goes in to save a child or a mother or a grandmother, then that's the risk that we run. We pull people out of burning buildings. We did it the other day, where we pulled a guy out, maybe five months ago, out of a burning building, right. Risking their [*sic*] lives, it's what we do, right?

Those people that are in that burning building, the only chance they have is you. The only chance they have for survival is how efficiently and how professionally you do your job. If they're not already deceased. But you know if they're viable, or if there's something, if they're savable, then you're their only chance.

It's nice to be recognized, but I don't know what the definition of hero is. We, the guys out here, do really dangerous, successful heroic deeds nearly every day.

So while heroism did not appear to resonate with either group of firefighters, the narratives of structural firefighters were often imbued with hero-like imagery. Interestingly, heroism also appeared at the level of the symbolic. Structural firefighters commissioned an artist to create a sculpture for veterans retiring from the force. The figure was a male firefighter carrying a small, apparently injured or unconscious child.

The central location of the main fire station, and the fact that structural firefighters fought the fire within the city limits, meant that they were more accessible to the media and, in turn, received more favourable coverage, including the cultivation of heroic masculinity. Ultimately the organization of firefighting efforts and the media's work as reputational entrepreneurs created a social milieu in which structural firefighters had some advantages over other groups; they were better positioned to stake a socially and culturally valid claim to heroic masculinity. But this position in the gender hierarchy had to be secured. In order to understand how this battle was waged and why structural firefighters prevailed, we must take a close look at the firefighters' narratives – their talk about the fire – and consider the ways in which their strategies were connected to masculinity dynamics.

Contesting Credibility

The discursive strategies that firefighters used in their attempts to reign supreme can be most broadly conceived as boundary work (Gieryn 1983); that is, the firefighters strengthened and reinforced occupational boundaries in an attempt to further distinguish their group from other groups. In carving out these borders, the firefighters attempted to effectively portray themselves as superior vis-à-vis those whom they constructed as Others. However, the work of constructing and maintaining occupational boundaries and creating superior selves was also an inherently gendered one. The firefighters' occupational boundaries mapped directly onto socially constructed boundaries that delineated the difference between "us" (the competent firefighters and real men) and "them" (the inferior firefighters and subordinate men). This process of identity construction, by which firefighters compared and judged those constructed as Others in order to position themselves as superior men, can be conceptualized as "gendered strategies of self" (Pacholok 2009, 476).

"Strategies of self" implies that this work is accomplished solely by individuals; however, they are also collective efforts that serve a collective end. A group effort is required to successfully create and enforce symbolic boundaries between those who are in – those who can legitimately claim a particular self – and those who are out (Schwalbe and Mason-Schrock 1996). In the case of the Mountain Park fire, communal work (including the work of the media) was required to effectively enforce and reinforce the boundaries that delineated those who could successfully claim to be the most competent and masculine firefighters.

The firefighters' gendered strategies of self entailed undermining the competence and credibility of those outside of their occupational group. They did so by wielding a measuring stick of firefighting efficacy that was variously deemed to include remaining calm in a crisis, using aggressive tactics, controlling emotions, and exterminating fire. These standards correspond directly to culturally dominant patterns of masculinity, which include imperatives for physical, mental, and emotional toughness; power and wealth; competitiveness; risk taking; the subordination of women; and the marginalization of gay men (Brannon 1976; Connell 1987; Goffman 1963; Kimmel 1994). As a result, using these gendered criteria for firefighting competence to evaluate Others simultaneously undermined the masculine integrity of the targeted group.

Calmness and Reliability in a Crisis

Both wildland and structural firefighters used narratives that constructed their group as the most level headed and unflappable in the face of the encroaching flames. According to Josh, the young wildland firefighter who earlier remarked that structural firefighters "got all the glory," wildland crew leaders were calm under pressure, while structural firefighters fell apart: "We had some [crew leaders] ... who have both seen huge fire. But nothing like this. And they were just rock solid. They said, 'No worries. Get in [the vehicles]. We'll get you all through.' Everybody else was panicked. Like the Kelowna Fire Department was just wiggy." One of the crew leaders to whom Josh was referring, Chris, explained that there were two occasions on which he instructed structural firefighters to leave an area for safety reasons and, owing to their ignorance of forest fire behaviour, they resisted. However, according to Chris, there had been other times that they "took off" when it was safe, which resulted in the loss of houses: "There were times when the structure guys again ... the times they would leave an area when it was safe, and then homes would go. And you'd say, 'Well, where the hell did they go?' So then you get on the radio and you start telling them, 'No, you guys, it is safe there. I know what the fire is doing, I know where it is, and I know what it's going to do. If you're there right now, you can save a couple.' But no, of course they weren't."

Structural firefighters used similar tactics to portray wildland firefighters in an unflattering manner. For example, one structural firefighter, Mark, delighted in relaying a story in which wildland firefighters apparently pulled back from the front line of the fire while the structural firefighters held their ground:

> And I remember we were up in the Rimrock area when the fire broke through ... So we're sitting there, and we know it's coming because you can hear it, the heat, the wind, the smoke, the dust, everything. The forestry guys, you know they're all in there. And then all of a sudden we heard these whistles. And that's an emergency signal for the forestry to get the hell out. So all of these whistles, you can just hear them going right across the mountainside, and we're kind of listening and then we're like what the hell is that? And it looked like rats jumping off a burning ship [chuckles]. These guys were running as hard as they could out of the forest, *by us*, and down the hill and they're gone. And we're sitting there going, "I think it's coming. You guys ready?" "Oh yeah!"

Mark's narrative positions his group as the competent firefighters, the "real" men who stayed to fight the fire. In contrast, according to Mark, the wildland firefighters ran away when things got bad. This implies that the structural firefighters were brave while others were not. Structural firefighters – rational, fearless, and calm under pressure – were ready to take on the fire, and ultimately, as Mark later claimed, it was these men who put it out.

Mark's story is especially potent given the occupational culture of structural firefighting, a culture in which running away is reprehensible. An upper-level administrator confided that it was difficult when structural firefighters had to retreat from the fire (presumably for safety reasons), because they felt like they were running away: "They had to pull out of [the fire zone]. And that's like running from something. And they're not used to running from anything. You know, like, even when it makes common sense, it just doesn't happen that often." In fact, running away is so scorned that one firefighter ended up on stress leave as a result: "You know, I'm not even privy to all of it, but I'm sure some of them ran, you know ... Like I know one that did. And he went off on stress leave. Like he just couldn't live with himself, eh? And I don't know if he'll ever be the same." Given this occupational imperative, to claim (as Mark did) that wildland firefighters ran away is a serious insult that directly undermines their credibility, both as firefighters and as men.

Aggression and Risk Taking

Firefighters from both camps also portrayed their group as the better firefighters by pointing to their aggressive firefighting tactics and the risks they took in their efforts to extinguish the flames. Greg, the supervisor who earlier criticized the media coverage of the fire, explained that it was actually his people who put themselves in harm's way: "While the fire department did a great job on the structure side of it, and I don't want to take anything away from anyone, anywhere on the structural side, but when it came to the actual front line of those fires and the people who put themselves at risk, it was our people under there."

In his explanation Greg discursively positions his crew (and himself, by association) as the real firefighters, the men who put themselves at risk and got the job done. One wildland firefighter went public with this claim, stating that structural firefighters "disappeared" when the blaze was burning near his property: "I hate to be cynical, but I don't have a good word to say about them. You need passion and adrenalin to fight a fire. Their tolerance of risk was minimal" (Poulsen 2003). The Kelowna fire chief vehemently denied these accusations, and after an internal review an upper-level manager from the BC Ministry of Forests issued an apology, which was reported in the local media. Many structural firefighters also talked about the perils associated with their job; however, they tended to view risk and danger as an everyday part of their duties, which was revealed in their discourse about heroism. In both cases, the implication is that firefighting competence requires taking risks, and, implicitly, those who are willing to take those risks are the most masculine.

Repudiating the Feminine

"Identity lies in difference; and difference is asserted against what is closest, that which represents the greatest threat" (Bourdieu 1984, 479). In like fashion, undermining masculinity is often achieved by implying that the person in question has qualities associated with femininity (for example see Iacuone 2005). Tellingly, firefighters distanced themselves from stereotypically feminine attributes and inferred that other firefighters were incompetent by associating them with femininity. These gendered strategies of self worked simultaneously to bolster the masculine credibility of the narrator and his colleagues and to undermine the masculinity of the out-group in question. Ultimately, delineating "real" and appropriately gendered firefighters from Others, and thereby marginalizing those who were perceived as threats, was an attempt to secure a place at the top of the gender hierarchy.

One veteran structural firefighter, Richard, who had recently moved into an administrative position, explained the differences between structural and wildland firefighters in the following way:

> [The wildland firefighters'] job is more containment. Structural firefighters are aggressive; we don't take loss very well. Forestry firefighters are more tactical; they're more like army guys. They're willing to take some losses to get some gains, if that makes sense to you? I mean, they're willing to give up a hundred acres of wildland and burn it themselves to stop the fire. Where we would never burn the house down to save another house. We would try and save that house and we would try and save the other house. That's the mental make-up of a structural firefighter versus a forestry guy, right. Forestry guys are like, "Okay, we'll build a guard here of dirt, and then we'll burn all this off so it doesn't come here, right. So we'll sacrifice some to get some." Where structural firefighters are not about sacrificing anything.

Here structural firefighters are portrayed as aggressive, uncompromising, and unwilling to lose, and forestry firefighters as less aggressive, even passive, and prepared to give up ground (at least some of the time). This rhetoric positions structural firefighters as better firefighters, while equating the "mental make-up" of wildland firefighters with "feminine" characteristics like passivity. Richard points to the firefighting tactics that are specific to each occupation and uses these as resources to construct the competence and masculinity of structural firefighters as superior to that of wildland firefighters. It is also noteworthy that while Richard compares wildland firefighters to "army guys," who are typically associated with aggressive masculinity (Jeffreys 2007), the comparison suggests otherwise here, where the army was largely cast as support workers brought in for the ignoble job of mop-up duty.

In like fashion, wildland firefighters indicated that they had a more difficult job and worked under more challenging conditions than did structural firefighters. They proclaimed that they worked for weeks to contain large fires, using very little water, and with far fewer tools than structural firefighters had. Here, Randy, a forestry officer who supervised wildland firefighters during the fire, explained that structural firefighters have a relatively simple job while wildland firefighters are charged with stopping a substantially more powerful force: "Fighting forest fires is nowhere near fighting a house fire, okay? Because when [structural firefighters] fight a house fire, what the main job is, other than get everybody out safe, for fire departments, is to keep it from spreading to the next-door neighbour's. That's it. They've got this 1,000, 2,000 square foot house burning in a block. They stop it from burning into other structures. That's what their primary function is. How can you stop something [such as a wildfire] that's moving a kilometre, you know, ... every ten seconds?"

In an ethnography of wildland firefighting, Desmond (2007, 130) insightfully advances the following argument to explain the wildland firefighters' claim to be the "real" firefighters: "Wildland firefighters do not enjoy the cultural prestige that structural firefighters do. They do not wax their fire engines and cruise down the local parade route, lights flashing; they are not the subject of countless popular books and movies ... In retaliation, wildland firefighters claim authenticity ... [W]ildland firefighters classify structural firefighting as less authentic and more sissified." Not only were Other firefighters positioned as less aggressive, with an easier mandate, but they were constructed as emotionally weak. For example, several wildland firefighters pointed to the mental state of structural firefighters and to an emotional display by the fire chief, in a way that challenged the masculinity of structural firefighters. In a well-publicized statement to the media the fire chief broke down in tears while relaying the events of Black Friday. On numerous occasions wildland firefighters mentioned this event even though I did not enquire about it. The chief's emotions, or "crocodile tears" as several called them, were depicted in a derogatory manner. Most emotions, with the exception of anger, are equated with femininity (Bird 1996; Rubin 2004) and, therefore, are something to be disparaged. Wildland firefighters' accounts revealed disdain for public displays of emotion, and their caustic remarks called into question the fire chief's masculinity.

Gender Hegemony: Power, Struggle, and Consequences

One could advance a number of perfunctory explanations for these struggles over credibility and firefighting supremacy. Perhaps wildland firefighters engaged in this dialogue because they felt unsupported and abandoned by the media and the public; thus they attempted to rescue their dignity and self-esteem because they had marginal standing on the status hierarchy. Pointing to structural firefighters' "lack" of firefighting skills gave wildland firefighters some leverage in their claim to superiority because, as Lamont (2000, 111) explains, "by subordinating social status to what they perceive to be the 'real' value of a person, workers create the possibility of locating themselves at the top of the hierarchy." However, this is only part of the story, one that does not consider the tenuous nature of gender construction. As masculinity is fragile and contested (Connell 1995; Kimmel 1994), it must constantly be proven (Kaufman 2001). The talk of wildland firefighters reveals that not only were they attempting to rescue their dignity and self-esteem, but they were also working to resurrect their masculinity.

And what of structural firefighters? Why were the men who were held up as heroes engaged in a struggle for credibility and firefighting dominance? Perhaps they had to justify the praise they had received because they felt that they had not actually won the battle against the fire. As one rookie explained, "it was hard to believe that the public was behind us at that time. Because we hadn't done our job – I didn't feel." Structural firefighters were at the top of the status hierarchy, but in order to stay there they had to prove that they deserved it. There were, however, less obvious masculinity dynamics that explain the structural firefighters' desire to prove that they were, in fact, deserving of the accolades they had received.

Both wildland and structural firefighting masculinities closely paralleled hegemonic masculinity, which cannot be reduced to a simple model of cultural control (Connell 1995; Connell and Messerschmidt 2005). As Monaghan (2002, 530) stresses, "male hierarchy is never static or guaranteed; it is processual, contested and requires the continual … (re)production of situational dominance, authority and subordination." Since one's position at the top of gendered status hierarchies is always contested, ascendancy is never guaranteed, and a great deal of effort is required to maintain positioning. So even those with power are compelled to engage in practices that refute the integrity of those they construct as Others. The structural firefighters, then, had to work continuously to maintain their status vis-à-vis other firefighters and to prove that they were, in fact, the better men. They reinforced the boundary between themselves and Others by discursively positioning wildland firefighters as less competent and, implicitly, as less manly. The non-structural firefighters contested the structural firefighters' claims and also portrayed themselves as worthy of merit by claiming exemplary masculinity. However, the odds were stacked against them, owing in part to the physical location of their work, the media coverage of the fire, and their ongoing public relations issues. As a result, the wildland firefighters' claims to superior masculinity were largely unsuccessful in the end.

The collective actions of the media bounded the parameters of heroic masculinity, which validated the structural firefighters' gendered strategies of self in ways that bolstered their credibility as firefighters and as masculine (even heroic) men. The boundary work of the media also provided structural firefighters with a status shield (Tracy and Scott 2006) that enabled them to avoid criticism for the losses, in ways that other firefighters could not.

The firefighters could have told different stories or drawn on different explanations for these events. For example, the structural firefighters could have argued that the wildland firefighters were younger and less experienced, or even less professional, to explain their apparent lack of aggression. Similarly, the wildland firefighters could have pointed out that structural firefighters simply have different training and responsibilities, which could explain their uneasiness in some situations. Instead, the firefighters inferred the Others as "sissies" through gendered emotional and behavioural indirects (for example, fearful behaviour, displays of emotion, passivity), implying that their group was the most competent in terms of firefighting and masculinity, while other firefighters were less so. This is especially telling since the firefighters were not queried about the competence of other firefighting groups. In fact, it was a topic that I tried to avoid because of the lawsuit in the works at the time of the interviews, and my promise to gatekeepers that in my research I would not point fingers or place blame for the losses.

The fact that structural firefighters, the group with the most power and status, used these strategies at all is a clear indication that dominant masculinities are not statically reproduced but are always contested. This instability also means that dominant patterns of gender practice are subject to change or undoing, a point to which I return below.

The firefighters did not appear to be cognisant of their strategies of self, likely because boundaries are often reinforced in the unnoticed habits and language of everyday life (Fuchs Epstein 1992). Further, as Sherman (2005) insightfully observes, strategy does not necessarily imply an intentional or explicit act (referring to Bourdieu 1990); rather, strategies may be anything that is functional to a worker's interest in establishing superiority. Despite the possible lack of intention, the effects of boundary work and strategies that elevated one's own status at the expense of others were no less pernicious.

Penalties and Rewards

The fire and its aftermath was a difficult experience for many firefighters, and there were long-term consequences for some. At least one firefighter had resigned, one senior member had retired shortly after the fire, and the fire chief had retired two years later (at the age of fifty-six). Several firefighters were on stress leave at the time of the interviews, some were having marital difficulties, a number were on medication to reduce stress, and a least two senior firefighters had been diagnosed with post-traumatic stress disorder. There were also a handful of firefighters who had chosen to leave their jobs a year or more after the fire, citing the fire as one reason for their decision. It appears, in the words of the fire chief, that this fire did have a "bad effect" on many of the firefighters. At least some of these effects were related to the gendered strategies of self that the firefighters employed in their efforts to attain superior status and reinforce occupational and symbolic boundaries.

Barrett (1996, 141) notes that these strategies also result in a catch-22 that does not bode well for establishing a stable sense of masculinity: "Preoccupation with differentiating self and discounting others creates an enduring sense of subjective insecurity. This persistent sense of fragility and precariousness generates a greater need to display worth. Such defensive posturing – differentiating self by out-performing others, validating self by negating others – is not only unlikely to lead to the achievement of a secure identity, it creates the very social conditions that drive men to strive for a chance to demonstrate exceptionality." This social irony played out in like fashion after the fire. Firefighters' strategies sustained the very disparities about which those at the bottom of the hierarchy were so incensed, namely that they did not get the respect and recognition that they felt they so rightly deserved, which in turn fuelled their ongoing quest to prove masculine superiority.

There was a collective sense of failure among the firefighters, yet in the end some of those who had "failed" (that is, the structural firefighters) emerged as victors. If the credibility of the wildland firefighters was under siege solely because valuable resources had been lost to the flames, the structural firefighters would have been subjected to the same criticism. However, quite the opposite occurred: structural firefighters escaped public condemnation,[1] were held up as heroes, and were showered with praise and rewards. What really mattered for the outcome of this credibility contest was the ability to declare firefighting competence and superior masculinity.

The firefighters who were unable to make this declaration faced a number of penalties. First, they were denied many of the symbolic and material rewards that the structural firefighters received. Second, because the wildland firefighters were relatively unsuccessful in their quest to affirm exemplary masculinity, it is plausible that new possibilities were created for those who had been formerly passed over on the basis of gender (and potentially sexuality) to infiltrate their ranks. In contrast, the structural firefighters, with the help of the media, successfully defended the masculine boundaries of their occupation. Losing the battle but winning the war means that structural firefighters are better placed to defend future "threats" to the gender hierarchy in their organization. In addition, as hero status creates a sense of immunity from public scrutiny, these firefighters may feel little pressure to address broader social changes (Lewis 2004), such as the calls for gender equity in paid work. These dynamics will make it difficult for non-traditional aspirants to join their organization in the future.

Third, the loss of valuable resources and the symbolic battle over credibility resulted in a full-fledged credibility crisis for the wildland firefighters, the pilots, and their organization. I was not surprised to learn that several years after the fire a name alteration was implemented, changing the Protection Branch to the Wildfire Management Branch – a semantic shift signifying that wildfires are, for the most part, inevitable and therefore something to be managed (as opposed to stamped out in the name of protection). Current statements on the organization's website speak to the success of firefighters in containing wildfires ("92 percent of all wildfires in B.C. within the first 24-hours of discovery") as well as the challenges they face in doing so ("B.C.'s forests and wild-lands cover over 94 million hectares … [firefighters are] confronted by an average of 2,000 wildfires each year"). While their mandate mentions protection ("Protect British Columbia forest land, grass land, natural resources and other assets from unwanted wildfire"), it also implies that wildfires, especially interface fires, cannot be stopped all of the time: "The Wildfire Management Branch is tasked with managing wildfires on both Crown and private lands outside of organized areas such as municipalities or regional districts. While the Wildfire Management Branch is mandated to protect life and assets, particularly forests and grasslands, it gives high priority to fires in interface areas where communities and forests come together. As B.C.'s population continues to grow and more people build homes in or near wildland areas, the interface area will be the biggest challenge facing the Wildfire Management Branch" (BC Ministry of Forests, Wildfire Management Branch 2010a). The name change enables the organization and its employees, in the aftermath of losing (that is, "failing" to fully protect the resources under their stewardship), to package themselves as forest and wildfire managers, and it consequently works to repair their credibility crisis (and perhaps prevent further such crises).

Did this masculinity crisis create a space for gender change? Unfortunately, rather than subverting existing gender patterns, the struggles for dominance exacerbated the inequalities among the men and did nothing to unsettle the gender hierarchy. Instead, they created inter-group tension and conflicts, which the firefighters resolved by using gendered strategies of self that positioned some groups as superior (ultimately as more masculine) and others as subordinate. The standards invoked to define and demonstrate masculinity, including aggression, risk taking, and the suppression of emotions, entrenched the hegemony of this gender pattern and consequently shored up boundaries between groups.

While the fire had the unfortunate effect of solidifying inter-group factions, conflicts can create spaces for gender change. As Connell (2000a, 13) notes, "masculinities are often in tension, within and without. It seems likely that such tensions are important sources of change."

The possibilities for changing dominant patterns of gender practice may be greatest when men's interests are divided because the presence of hierarchies among men means that not all men benefit equally from patriarchy. Furthermore, most men share some common interests with women. Therefore, men are motivated to varying degrees to generate change in the gender order; it may be in the best interests of some men to challenge the status quo and of others to actively maintain or go along with it (Connell 2000a).

In the case of the Mountain Park fire, firefighters did not have a wholly collective interest in banding together to protect their privileges. Instead, they were actively involved in undermining the gender and occupational credibility of the firefighters from other groups, which effectively pitted groups of (mostly) men against one another. The firefighters were at odds with one another as never before. If Connell is right, this could be a catalyst for change in the gender regime of firefighting. Significantly, it was in this volatile context that men and women firefighters toiled side by side on the front lines of the fire, both working to demonstrate their proficiency under especially challenging conditions. In the following chapter I ask whether these pressures disrupted the gender relations in the firefighters' workplaces.

6 Working with the Other: Resistance, Accommodation, and Reproduction

Losing the battle against the Mountain Park fire, and the presence of a social hierarchy, presented challenges for the doing of gender in the firefighters' workplaces. However, these potential catalysts for gender change were largely contained via the structural organization of the firefighting efforts, the work of the media as reputational entrepreneurs, and the firefighters' discursive attempts to reconstruct themselves as competent and appropriately gendered workers. The picture revealed thus far is a relatively discouraging one for gender change. What remains to be examined, however, is the way in which the men reacted to the women firefighters who laboured by their side in a bid to halt the advancing flames.

Gender at Work in the Wake of Disaster

Empirical research on the construction of masculinities in blue-collar occupations demonstrates convincingly that these occupations are highly masculinized; that is, they represent the interests of men workers (or, at least, "appropriately" gendered men) (Acker 1990; Britton 1997; Williams 1995), and culturally valued ideals of masculinity are embedded in the meaning and practice of work (Desmond 2007). Much of this research also suggests that masculinity is constructed, reproduced, and more or less sustained in and through blue-collar work (for example see Barrett 1996; Catano 2003; Meyer 1999; Ouellet 1994; Quam-Wickham 1999; Sasson-Levy 2002) and that the entry of women and marginalized men into these occupations does little to challenge workplace gender relations (for example see Britton 2003; Chetkovich

1997; Enarson 1984; Paap 2006; Prokos and Padavic 2002; Yoder and Aniakudo 1997).

This literature paints a relatively bleak picture of gender change, suggesting that workplace masculinities are largely impervious to challenges and that women's presence is generally not disruptive to the gender regimes in these male-dominated spaces. Regrettably, the broader trend in gender theorizing to use "doing gender" as a theory of gender persistence has shaped the research on gender and work in ways that obfuscate the possibility of gender reform (Deutsch 2007) and, thus, the transformative potential of crisis events in these settings. Maier and Messerschmidt's (1998) study of the space shuttle *Challenger* disaster is an important exception to this pattern. The authors note that crises are times in which gender may be enacted in unconventional ways: "In certain [crisis] situations, men in organizations may actually engage in practices that are in opposition to more common, ideal-type masculine practices" (337). However, they ultimately conclude that while some men resisted the pressure to launch the shuttle and others did not (Messerschmidt 1995), both were doing masculinity in the re-productive sense.

Research on paid work has also been susceptible to the proclivity in the gender literature to overlook the agency of women in the construction of gender among men. As Connell and Messerschmidt (2005, 848) argue, we need to pay much closer attention to these gender dynamics: "... focusing only on the activities of men occludes the practices of women in the construction of gender among men ... Our understanding of hegemonic masculinity needs to incorporate a more holistic understanding of gender hierarchy, recognizing the agency of subordinated groups as much as the power of dominant groups."

It would be inaccurate to say that women, and the ways in which women enact gender, have been left out of the picture altogether. For a long while gender scholars have recognized that gender is constructed relationally; hegemonic masculinity is constructed in relation to femininity and other configurations of masculinity (Connell 2000a). To date, this theoretical insight has primarily played out at the level of the symbolic and has not been extended to include the gender practices of actual women. Sered (1999, 194) makes the following epistemological distinction between the symbolic construct "Woman" and the lives of actual women, in a discussion of gender and religion: "The first [issue] centers on women – that is, actual people who have varying degrees of agency within specific social situations. Women as agents can demand rights, enter into negotiations, and protest unfair treatment ... The second set of issues centers on Woman – a symbolic construct conflating gender, sex, fantasy, and ... men's psychological projections" (emphasis original).

The relationship between Woman as an ideological and cultural representation and women as material subjects is one of the central questions that feminists seek to address (Mohanty 1991). Relational approaches primarily examine workplace masculinity construction in relation to Woman, that is, the way masculinity is practised in contrast to the way femininity is symbolically configured. What is often missing is "women," the daily lived realities and practices of actual, embodied women. Consequently, women's agency, and its influence on gender practices among men, is also left under-theorized. These relational dynamics, Martin (2001, 589) argues, are ignored in mainstream organizational theories, which tend to "focus on masculinities from men's standpoint(s) and to ignore women except as object of men's actions ... Studies of men *from women's standpoint* are thus rare in organizational research ... Yet, approaching the subject in this way can reveal dynamics that are ignored by mainstream organizational theories (and descriptions) and illuminate how gender affects workplaces through interactions and interpretations between sexes" (emphasis original).

Excluding women from research on masculinities and work is also problematic if the goal is to move beyond examinations of gender persistence towards incidents of gender disruption. "Real" women are much more troublesome for gender reproduction (that is, for doing gender as replication) because women have agency; they act, they are corporeally present, and they can challenge, subvert, and deny. They are more than signs or symbols of femininity ready to be cognitively manipulated, selectively invoked, or read in ways that provide a seamless foil against which masculinities are constructed. Rather, women – more, women's agency – can disrupt the doing of gender by men. Thus, we must heed the call to include women's agency in order to better theorize the ways in which gender is destabilized at work.

Theories of gender doing and undoing also imply an audience. Not inconsequentially, one's audience can minimize the extent to which agency is effective. In West and Zimmerman's (1987) theory, audience is theorized in the form of accountability; gender is performed with and for an audience (actual or virtual) that holds one accountable to "proper" norms of conduct for one's sex category. Similarly, Nentwich (2008) argues that audiences can enforce gender norms and the binaries on which they are predicated. Audiences, then, have the power to resist, dilute, or deny actors' attempts to unsettle the gender order. "Subversive practices and discourses are always in danger of being domesticated by the dominant logic, and their success always depends on the audience interpreting the act under question" (226). Rebellious gender performances only constitute a challenge to hegemonic gender practices if the audience interprets it in that way, but the same act could be interpreted in ways that reify the binary (Nentwich 2008). Women's agency, then, is not omnipotent, because one's audience can reconfigure the message in ways not intended by the actor. These theories suggest that while women's agency has the potential to interrupt the reproduction of workplace gender, there are no guarantees; the success of women's agency is ultimately contingent on the ways in which the audience engages with their performance. While gender is done for both real and virtual audiences, I propose that disruptions are more likely when real women are present.

In sum, broader trends in gender theorizing have influenced the research on gender and work in ways that obscure the possible mechanisms of gender resistance and reform and the disruptive potential of women's agency, especially in times of crisis. Based on the extant literature on doing gender and work, one would expect that gender would simply be reproduced when there are crises in male-dominated workplaces. I suggest that a more complex picture emerges when we theorize women's agency and audience reactions, one that reveals spaces in which patterns of hegemonic gender practice begin to unravel, even in the most masculine of occupations.

Interface Fire as a Proving Ground

Not only did the Mountain Park fire require men firefighters to work alongside their female counterparts, but both were labouring in the most difficult of fire configurations, an interface fire. When asked whether there were any special issues that arose in an interface fire, Greg, a seasoned veteran in the forest service, noted that working on such a fire was especially intense: "I think whenever you throw something like that into the mixture, um – when you go out and fight a fire that's just out in the timber and then you throw a house on top of it – oh yeah, that's a whole different element, absolutely. There's no doubt that – I think the adrenalin flows a lot more when you start throwing

Figure 6.1 Women on the fire line (photograph by Cory Bialecki)

an interface fire – you throw a house and livestock, and all that goes in that, oh yeah, it throws a whole different atmosphere to it."

Firefighters undergo extensive training; however, a real fire is an important occasion for demonstrating competence, and a job well done garners the trust and respect of co-workers. This is especially true in the case of an interface fire, which is a particularly intense event because multiple structures and the forest are burning simultaneously. Here, Nathan, a rookie structural firefighter, explains how the Okanagan Mountain fire provided an opportunity to show his senior colleagues that he could perform under pressure:

> When you come on as a new guy, you're trained and everything but the guys don't really – they trust you, but until you've been in a situation with them, that's when the team gels, and the morale, and everything else. So for us [rookies], [the fire] was probably the best thing that could have happened to us because we were right alongside everybody during this, and there wasn't, you know – we're still probationary and we're still junior, but you kind of went through something with just about everybody ... So that was a positive for us ... they trust you ... they've seen you, you're not scared to go in somewhere, you're gonna, you know – because that's what everyone thinks about if I go in: "I don't know this new guy. Is he gonna have my back if something goes wrong?"

The fire was an important proving ground for men, but it also presented unprecedented opportunities for women to demonstrate their skill and competence on the largest interface fire in British Columbia's history. So how did women take up this challenge? What implications did their actions have for the construction of gender among their male colleagues? Did the men continue to accomplish gender in relatively conventional ways or did they rework gender in ways that challenged gender hierarchies? In the case of the latter, under what conditions did women's efforts destabilize gendered patterns of practice? To begin, I take a close look at women firefighters' agency – their efforts to resist the status quo – followed by men firefighters' reflections on the efforts of their women colleagues.

Women Firefighters Navigating Othering: Agency and Resistance

Demonstrating Competence on the Fire Line

Women who enter male-dominated, blue-collar occupations must work exceptionally hard to demonstrate that they are competent workers (Britton 2003; Chetkovich 1997; Martin 1994; Padavic 1991; Yoder and Aniakudo 1997). For women firefighters, proving themselves constituted both acquiescing and resisting (in varying degrees) to the decidedly masculine culture of their workplaces. Sherry, in her fourth season as a unit crew firefighter, navigated this space by going to great lengths to demonstrate her competence in firefighting tasks. Here she conveys a story about building a make-shift bridge and about her ongoing efforts to achieve credibility during the fire in the face of paternalism from her co-workers and outright disdain from heavy equipment operators:

> So we had two [chain] saws. And [one of the guys] was running one of the saws, and then the other guy – there was another guy who was doing the planning part of the bridge or whatever, and he had faller's pants.[1] And it was going pretty slow with just the one saw, but he was just supposed to be doing the planning. So I asked if I could grab his pants just to, you know, [cut] up logs. So he was like, "Are you sure?" you know. So I, you know, put on his faller pants and I've got his saw. And there's the [heavy equipment operators] and this guy, and then there's our squad. And these three guys, they actually asked me if I knew what I was doing with the saw. They asked me if I was qualified: "Are you allowed to run the saw?"

Not all firefighters are permitted to use the chainsaw. Cutting trees is viewed as a highly skilled and enjoyable task; only those deemed worthy are assigned this coveted job. Sherry's agency – her desire to show her co-workers that she was an adept firefighter – could not have been more obvious than when she literally took the pants off her colleague so that she could use the chainsaw to cut up logs. Her effort – more, her *work* – was required on an ongoing basis, from the moment she met new colleagues at the beginning of each season to every time she came in contact with a different crew: "You have to prove yourself every time."

Sherry was also treated in a condescending fashion by co-workers who offered help based on the assumption that she did not know how to operate small engines (even though such equipment is an integral part of firefighting). Sherry actively resisted this stereotype by discursively positioning herself as equally, if not more, skilled at operating equipment than were her male co-workers. In the following passage she relays an incident about starting a chainsaw.

> So I'm sitting there and I'm pulling it, and like this guy starts walking over to me like he's gonna start it for me, and I'm just like, "go away," you know. It's that whole thing that if it was another guy, they'd never dream of doing that. And they hover around you and they give you advice and

watch your every move ... It's the same with the pumps: if you have breasts you can't start the pump [laughs]. I'm probably better on the pump and like small engines and stuff than half the guys on the crew ... It just irritates me because I'm just like "out of my way, I know what I'm doing!" [laughs]

The fire provided Sherry with an unprecedented opportunity to challenge the gender hierarchy in her workplace, and through the successful accomplishment of her tasks she threatened to destabilize the link between firefighting and the imperative for a masculine, male body. Sherry's colleague, Kathy, had a somewhat different strategy for making her way in this masculine occupational milieu.

Neutralizing Gender

Kathy, a relatively well-seasoned wildland firefighter who had several people working under her, also toiled on the front lines of the fire alongside men colleagues. She minimized the salience of gender at work by stressing that she was not different from her colleagues; she saw herself as a firefighter first. Moreover, she saw herself as a genderless firefighter. So when I asked her what it was like to be the only woman on her crew, she struggled to answer: "It's kind of a hard question to actually answer just because I've never really felt different from – I mean, on this base I've never really felt different that I'm a female. I'm a firefighter, and it's sort of like that whole thing when you say, 'Hey, you guys.' I mean I don't care if they call me guys, girls; I mean it's one [and] the same ... I apologize because people have asked me this before and I really can't give them a fair answer because I don't think that my gender has anything to do with my ability to fight fire."

In her attempt to carve out a discursive space in which gender is irrelevant, Kathy did not mind contending with what many would view as sexist language; in her mind, guys and girls were "one and the same." The power and omnipresence of gender are erased through her dialogue. Male nouns signify power and authority in ways that female nouns do not (it is not hard to imagine that men firefighters would react negatively to "Hey, you girls"). In addition, being called a guy would suggest that Kathy is part of the group, she fits in, and fitting in is important for success in highly masculinized workplaces like those of firefighting (Enarson 1984; Lewis 2004). Fitting in is also gendered; not only do women in these workplaces have to fit into the existing gender regime (largely a man's world), but they also must do so in a way that an appropriately gendered man would. As Chetkovich (1997, 15) notes, "men must prove they can be firefighters; women must prove they can – in some sense – be men."

Fitting in through the successful accomplishment of gender also bestows workplace proficiency upon the bearer. Given these dynamics, it is not difficult to see why Kathy discounts gender. This strategy situates her as one who fits in with her colleagues and, by effectively erasing femininity, it confers firefighter competence. Although this is my interpretation, not Kathy's, the fact that she deliberately makes note that her gender is not related to her firefighting abilities suggests that she is at least liminally aware (Martin 2003) of these processes.

While her attempts to make gender invisible provide Kathy with some advantages, constructing gender in this way also presents some dangers. Kathy is not truly a genderless firefighter, because in her line of work this worker is a man. As Acker (1990, 150) argues, "the concept of a universal worker excludes and marginalizes women who cannot, almost by definition, achieve the qualities of a real worker because to do so is to become like a man." While Kathy cannot become a man, she, like women in other male-dominated fields, can construct herself as a "conceptual man" at the cost of denying or repressing her femininity (Ranson 2005, 150).

Kathy continued to minimize gender during the remainder of the interview and explained that she did not want to use the term *male dominated* to explain the prevalence of men in her occupation: "The numbers are a lot more male, the ratio. I don't want to use the word *dominated* because I don't – I think that's sort of an overtone of, you know – I don't think it's domination at all ... but it's more men than women." Kathy actively resists the notion that she is dominated; from her perspective there are simply more men than women in her profession. However, neutralizing gender in this way also obfuscates the inequalities embedded in firefighters' workplaces. Kathy did not appear to make the connection between the lack of women firefighters and the masculine ideologies and practices in her workplace. However, when I said, "It sounds like you've never been made to feel like gender is an issue," she responded, "I, yeah, perhaps I have, but I refuse to let it, I guess. So I just – I can only control what I think, not what other people think." Again, Kathy asserts agency by refusing to let gender become an issue, at least in her mind, but she also recognizes the presence of gender and indicates that her co-workers may too.

Sherry's attempts to demonstrate competence are potentially more revolutionary. While Kathy and Sherry take individualized approaches to a larger structural problem, Sherry's approach is more deliberate and more visible. Sherry is especially resolute in her efforts, going out of her way to take on the most challenging tasks despite a lack of support from her immediate colleagues. She also firmly rejects the help offered by men colleagues – a very different strategy than that of forestry women who accept assistance in an effort to "demonstrate ability without giving offence" (Enarson 1984, 69). In contrast to Kathy, Sherry does not simply try to fit in by using discursive sleights of hand; rather, she positions herself as different from (that is, better than) her male colleagues and takes action to prove it. In a highly masculinized occupation like wildland firefighting these micro-level, seemingly trivial acts of everyday resistance (Gramsci 1971) are noteworthy.

When thinking about resistance, it is also useful to distinguish between strategies and tactics. Strategies, according to de Certeau (1984), are the ways in which dominant institutions attempt to control time and space. Drawing on this work, DeVoss (2002) differentiates between strategies and tactics, the latter conceptualized as actions "used by the weak to exploit tiny fissures, to exploit the possibilities of resistance" (85). Both Kathy and Sherry asserted agency in the face of the organizational strategies that largely maintained the gender regime in their workplace. However, Sherry's attempts to subvert that regime are more readily conceptualized as deliberate tactics.

The Audience: "There's Extra Attention Paid to You"

The presence of Sherry and Kathy and their efforts on the fire line did not go unnoticed; there were men in the audience who were witness to their work. For example, Sherry noted that she and her female colleagues were subjected to close surveillance. Much to her chagrin, "when we first picked [the saw] up, you can bet they watched us ... There's extra attention paid to you." Women's competent performance of masculine-coded jobs weakens the link with masculinity (Prokos and Padavic 2002); however, the success of practices in disrupting gender is contingent on the ways in which the audience interprets the acts in question. Thus, while women's skill on the fire line is potentially subversive, it is necessary to consider the ways the men in the audience constructed this work. It is to these colleagues that I now turn, asking, Did the presence of competent women firefighters, and their efforts to resist subordination, have implications for the ways in which their male colleagues constructed gender?

Accommodation and Reproduction

Women as Skilled Workers and Gender Deviants

Although structural firefighters in the Kelowna Fire Department did not usually work side by side with female firefighters, the Mountain Park fire provided an occasion for interaction with paid and volunteer firefighters from other departments, some of whom were women. Here, Rick, a veteran with the Kelowna Fire Department, recounts his experience with a woman structural firefighter:

> There were some gals up [at the fire]. Now they were all [structural] volunteers, from around the province ... On the Friday night, I was lucky, and I'll tell you that. She was a female, and if you give me a minute, I'll think of where she's from. But she was an assistant chief of a volunteer department. And she's a little, short, she was just as wide as she was tall, right? And she really impressed me. Because like I say, you had to see this fire. And these guys, when we went back in there, I think they looked at me like I had six heads. And then when plan A failed, and then when I came up with plan B, they were not gonna do it. And there's all these males, and this little chicken – and she was, I think, an assistant chief – she went in there. And I have bad language when I get mad, and I'm going, "Holy crap!" She went up one side of these guys and down the other and told them that if they didn't listen and do exactly what they're told by me – you know, and I'm just wow. And she was a female, and that's not – I think most females are great. There was lots of assistant chiefs, males, that were there, but she was the one that stepped up to the plate. And I think all the rest of the males were, " Holy crap, we're not gonna mess with her."

Rick simultaneously praises his colleague and marginalizes her. He felt "lucky" and pleasantly surprised that a woman firefighter (insultingly described as a "chicken") took charge. Clearly he was impressed; not only was she a volunteer firefighter (viewed as less skilled and trained than paid firefighters), but she was also a woman. He also notes that she was the one who got firefighters to follow orders when they would not listen to him. Rick was astounded not only by her assertiveness but also by her language. Moreover, it is no accident that he chose to describe her body, that "she was just as wide as she was tall." His dialogue implies that she was not "feminine" in body or in spirit but, in fact, was a gender anomaly. Rick's appraisal of his colleague is of somebody who got the job done under very difficult conditions, but his narrative also positions her as an unusual woman because he suggests that few women could accomplish what she did.[2]

In a similar fashion, Duncan, a wildland firefighter who supervised Sherry's crew, applauded the skill of the women in his group, at the same time constructing them as different from most women. When asked if women changed workgroup dynamics, Duncan stated that the crew had improved tremendously with the arrival of women, who were "very organized" and "put out a lot of effort" to better the crew. They also cleaned things up, both literally (the work trucks) and figuratively (the "male literature" disappeared). Duncan further elaborated:

> [Having women on the crew] makes a big difference. I mean, again, I had some pretty tough girls. They work just as hard as the guys do, if not harder. Like, they don't like people carrying anything for them; they won't let you carry anything for them. They don't like to be segregated [in camp]. I mean, realistically you've got your own tents anyway. I mean, everybody respects everybody's privacy. Again, they're – at least from my perspective, they fit in quite well. Again, you know, you're going to have your 20 per cent who feel like, "Why is she running the saw, and not me?" "Because she's better!" [laughter] and that's exactly what I tell them. "You just weren't good enough." You know, it might sound mean or however it comes off to them. It's just to put a point out there. It doesn't matter who you are; anybody can run the chainsaw.

Even though Duncan supports the presence of women on the crews, his discourse portrays competent women as exceptions to the norm, which has the unfortunate effect of undermining the credibility of his women colleagues. Since the "girls" didn't want special treatment, they were "tough" (that is, gender exceptions).

Portraying women colleagues as gender anomalies allows firefighters to preserve male privilege and the guise of workplace equality, while working side by side with women whose mere presence threatens the prestige of their work (Fuchs Epstein 1992) and its equation with masculinity (Padavic 1991). At the same time, one cannot ignore the praise they direct at these same women, by no means a trivial act in the masculine milieu of firefighting. Moreover, Duncan's statement that "anybody can run the chainsaw" effectively mutes gender differences because it implies that both (tough) women and men are capable of this task.

The effect of women's agency is also notable in theoretical terms. It is true that men define and perform masculinity for, and in relation to, other men (Kimmel 1994, 1996) and in opposition to symbolic constructs of women and femininity: "At times, it is not women as corporeal beings, but the 'idea' of women, or femininity – and especially a perception of effeminacy by other men – that animates men's actions. Femininity, separate from actual women, can become a negative pole against which men define themselves" (Kimmel 1996, 7). While much research has demonstrated that men must prove their manhood to other men, and in opposition to femininity and the symbolic Woman (Sered 1999), this case study of the Mountain Park fire also reveals that women's physical presence and actions, not simply ideas about women and gender, create pressure to modify existing gender scripts. Much previous theorizing and research on masculinity overlooks this subversive potential of women's actions (Connell and Messerschmidt 2005).

Making Gender Invisible

Men firefighters also diminished the differences between women and men by rendering gender irrelevant. As noted above, Kathy asserted her agency by neutralizing gender. In a somewhat similar strategy, Kathy's supervisor, Dave, a long-time veteran of the forest service, constructed *all* his charges as genderless workers: "We had Gail out there [on the fire], we had Kathy out there, digging the guard, doing their thing, and they're doing it as a worker, not necessarily as a woman. The other guys are doing it as a worker, not necessarily as a man." In this statement, the firefighters are constructed as workers, period, not gendered workers. As Acker (1990) notes, workers are implicitly men; however, Dave refutes this when he states that the men are also genderless. This is a more profound shift than is the claim made by Kathy, which implied that only women were genderless. Dave claims that both the men and the women are working as non-gendered beings; in the heat and the smoke of the fire line, where tremendous physical exertion is crucial to success, gender differences disintegrate much like trees in a raging fire.

Shortly after neutralizing gender, Dave pointed to male dominance to explain sexist images of women and asserted that warnings about harassment in the United States were " too much"; however, he quickly noted that he was proud of his female colleagues' accomplishments: "Now we get some stupidity out there where we get the – because of dominance of male we still have stuff like this [pointing to a large beer advertisement containing a scantily clad woman near his desk], yet if you were down in the U.S.A. on a fire, oh man, they just drill you [about] harassment and everything. And it's almost too much. And where we – I'm proud [we have] the only [woman] crew leader in the province that we're aware of. The other thing I'm proud of is [BC's having] the only woman fire chief in Canada." His picture objectifies women, yet he applauds the accomplishments of women firefighters. The tensions in his dialogue are palpable: he denies the salience of gender when he invokes the genderless worker, but he also acknowledges male dominance. In the end, his discursive attempt to render gender invisible is not entirely successful.

For the men firefighters the predominant pattern of gender practice was to both praise and marginalize their women colleagues and the work they did on the fire. Their narratives reveal, on the one hand, that they made some accommodations for the fact that the women with whom they worked were skilled and resistant to gender inequality. On the other hand, these men were reluctant to give up masculine privilege entirely, which was apparent when they undermined their women co-workers.

Interaction as a Site of Change: Doing, Undoing, and Redoing Gender

The talk of the women firefighters illustrates that they were actively engaged in navigating the gender tensions in their workplaces. Kathy did so by discursively neutralizing gender, while Sherry asserted that she was more competent at the firefighting tasks than were her male colleagues. Deutsch (2007) concludes that "doing gender" should be used to describe interactions that reproduce gender difference, and "undoing gender" should refer to interactions that reduce or eliminate gender differences. Using this criterion, one could conclude that Kathy is undoing gender and Sherry is doing gender, but I contend that this distinction is too tidy. Sherry positioned herself as different from her male colleagues on the grounds that she was better at symbolically *masculine* tasks. In this case, stressing difference does not necessarily equate to doing gender if doing gender is meant to reference gender stasis.

One could also argue that Sherry was doing alternative femininity by expanding the boundaries of stereotypical femininity to include practices traditionally associated with firefighting masculinity. This would not sit well with some, however. First, there are those who would argue that to constitute undoing gender, actions must not simply change the contents of the binary gender container but must disrupt the binary itself. Binaries create and sustain male privilege by justifying differential treatment and unequal resource allocation to women and men; thus, gender is only undone when these binaries are ruptured. Gender is undone when an audience interprets a subversive performance in a way that "troubles" the norm of binary distinctions between men and women (Nentwich 2008). Similarly, Lorber (2005) urges the dismantling of the binary gendered categories of men and women, and Risman (2009, 83) suggests that gender undoing occurs when the "essentialism of binary distinctions between people based on their sex category is challenged."

Risman also takes issue with the proclivity in gender research to label new and subversive behaviours as alternative masculinities or femininities simply because the group or person in question is biologically male or female. Subversive behaviours, she argues, destabilize the link between sex category and socially sanctioned masculine or feminine conduct and indicate that old gender norms are becoming less compelling. According to Risman, these kinds of behaviours constitute undoing gender.

Perhaps, then, what Sherry and Kathy are doing is the firefighting masculinity of the variety most highly rewarded in their workplace. Both Kathy and Sherry construct gender on masculine terms, Kathy implicitly by neutralizing and dismissing gender, and Sherry explicitly by claiming mastery over traditionally masculine tasks. In so doing, they demonstrate firefighting competence by practising appropriate workplace masculinity. Organizations are peopled by women and men who construct both femininities and masculinities (Liefbroer and Corijn 1999; Martin and Collinson 1999), and individual women can practise "masculinities" just as individual men can practice "femininities" (Connell 1995). Laying claim to and practising (especially for Sherry) firefighting masculinity disrupts the connection between sex category (woman) and gender (femininity). This, Risman would suggest, is undoing gender.

West and Fenstermaker (2002) indicate that although individuals are invariably held accountable to norms of womanly or manly behaviour, resistance may corrode the connection between specific actions and their corresponding sex category: "So, even as we as individuals may be held accountable (in relation to our character and motives) for our failure to live up to normative conceptions of gender, the accountability of *particular* conduct to sex category may thereby be weakened" (53–4; emphasis original). West and Zimmerman (2009) submit that what Risman is referring to is akin to redoing rather than undoing. They argue that while normative conceptions of femininity and masculinity may change, actors are nevertheless accountable to their sex category:

> Risman's remarks appear to treat gender as if it were anchored in a fixed set of specifications. This is what allows her to describe departures from the fixed set as an "undoing" of gender (a doing away with, as it were). It seems to us that what is involved in the matters she refers to is a change in the normative conceptions to which members of particular sex categories are held accountable. "Undoing" implies abandonment – that sex category … is no longer something to which we are accountable (i.e., that it makes no difference). That implication is one consequence of drawing from the concept of doing gender, without seeing that accountability sits at its core … Risman (2009) also speaks of a postgender society as "A just world … where sex category matters not at all beyond reproduction; economic and familial roles would be equally available to persons of any gender" (p. 84). But this implies that members of particular sex categories are accountable to (unspecified) reproductive issues. For us, this is a shift in accountability: Gender is not *undone* so much as *redone*. (117–18; emphasis original)

So, in the end, Sherry's and Kathy's performances most closely resemble redoing gender. They are accountable to their sex category by virtue of the fact that, as women, they are largely perceived as different from men (recognized by both themselves and their audience). Their individual acts do not disrupt male-female or masculine-feminine binaries. However, their agency – their physical work on the front lines of the fire – creates pressure to shift the normative standards to which they are held accountable.

Discussing interaction as a site of change, Deutsch (2007, 120) states that "by examining the effects of subversive action on its audience, we may be able to identify the conditions under which those actions change normative conceptions of gender." The men firefighters simultaneously validated the women and their work and undermined their efforts. On the one hand, the narratives of the men firefighters worked to marginalize their women colleagues by constructing them as gender anomalies and attempting to make workplace gender inequalities invisible. Thus, one might conclude that the men firefighters were doing gender. On the other hand, the tensions in the men's dialogue are a strong indication that the gender hierarchy was, in fact, destabilized by the women firefighters. For example, Duncan's statement that both women and men can operate a chainsaw (and his practice of ensuring that both did so) and Dave's claim that women and men are genderless on the fire line work to mute gender differences. In addition, it is clear that the men firefighters made some accommodations for women's agency by commending their work; in essence, they formulated a new gender discourse to account for women's actions. On this front, the work of women disrupted the doing of gender by men. This a hopeful sign of gender change.

Before declaring victory, though, we must further unpack the workings of gender and consider the way in which the hierarchy that created a rift among the men was connected to their motives for praising women firefighters. The Mountain Park fire created a struggle over symbolic and material resources that pitted men against one another along occupational lines. The firefighters' gendered strategies of self undermined the integrity of firefighters from other groups; they asserted that their own performance best exemplified firefighting excellence and masculinity and thus placed them (or should place them) at the top of a hierarchy of deserving firefighters. In the end, despite the fact that they were unable to prevent the destruction of hundreds of homes, the structural firefighters cemented their status as top-notch firefighters. The firefighters' gendered strategies of self, then, contributed to the wholesale reproduction of firefighting masculinity, despite the fact that it may have been in the best interests of some firefighters to disrupt this pattern of gender (a point to which I return in the concluding chapter).

In contrast to the adversarial relationships among the men, the women received accolades for their work and gained a certain measure of respect in their respective occupational circles. While this is promising, it is premature to conclude that gender inequities were eroded completely, as it is entirely plausible that firefighters' motives for praise were rooted in a non-progressive gender politics. I submit that one of the reasons the men praised their women colleagues was that they wanted to portray their occupational *group* as the most competent (and worthy of resources). This required them to applaud, rather than criticize, the work of their female co-workers.

"In certain situations men's relationships with particular women ... define interests that are stronger than their shared interests as men. In all these ways men's general interest in patriarchy becomes incoherent or contestable" (Connell 2000a, 32). In the case of the Mountain Park fire, firefighters were interested in sustaining their shared investment in patriarchy with other men, but they were also very invested in reinforcing occupational boundaries and constructing their own group as the best firefighters, which would allow them to secure more proximate resources. In their attempts to accomplish this, they highlighted the proficiency of the women on their crews.

In all probability, men firefighters wanted the best of both worlds – to situate themselves as different from and better than the men in other groups *and* as different from their women colleagues. However, the latter task was much more difficult to accomplish because during this fire the women were working side by side with the men, clearly visible and obviously up to the task. Women's agentive work took hold because it was visible to their male audience and because the men firefighters were at odds with one another. In the end, the women firefighters derived some benefits from the competition between men, which may bode well for cross-gender equality. In the final chapter I consider the implications of these findings for gender relations broadly, for theorizing about gender, and for future research on gender, disasters, and change.

7   Out of the Ashes

"When men show a willingness to assume equal responsibility in feminist struggle, performing whatever tasks are necessary, women should affirm their revolutionary work by acknowledging them as comrades in struggle." (hooks 2000)

The project began with a focus on gender instability and change. I have proposed that crises like the Mountain Park fire disrupt the mundane and, thus, have the potential to destabilize gender relations. I have identified several crisis tendencies that made the regular day-to-day doing of gender problematic, and I have made the case that these tensions could be catalysts for gender change. Specifically, I suggested that widespread damage to property and valuable resources troubled the notion that current configurations of firefighting masculinity were necessary for success and threatened to rupture the link between proficient firefighting and masculinity. I also concluded that the social hierarchy between firefighting groups positioned structural firefighters as heroes and non-structural firefighters as undeserving Others, which in turn rekindled animosities among men and undermined potential alliances among them. Finally, I indicated that the fire provided women firefighters (some in leadership roles) with an opportunity to prove themselves on the front lines of a rank-six wildfire, which imperilled the organizational rationales for excluding women and the gender foundation on which those claims rested.

Case studies of these crises revealed that even one year after the last embers had been extinguished, the gender tensions that had been generated by the disaster continued to smoulder. Each of these tensions endangered the status quo and necessitated a great deal of damage control on the part of the firefighters who had to stake renewed claims to firefighting masculinities and develop new strategies to "justify" patriarchy. While these firefighters were engaged in a physical battle to save homes and forest from the flames, they were also engrossed in a symbolic rescue of equal significance – the salvaging of firefighting masculinity and the privileges associated with it.

Patriarchy under Pressure

Crisis tendencies may result in new, more egalitarian patterns of masculinity, but patriarchy can also absorb the challenges posed by crises and result in the reproduction of gender inequalities. Posed at the outset of this study, these questions remain unanswered: Did the firefighters' strategies for negotiating the fire-related crises disrupt gender? Did the attempts of the firefighters to resolve these tensions further entrench the gender regimes of firefighting? Did they shift gender relations in ways that constituted gender undoing?

In the end, the ways in which each firefighting group attempted to absorb the challenge of losing did little to disrupt the gender regimes of firefighting or the patterns of masculinity that upheld them. It was not simply that the firefighters were unaccustomed to losing and this fuelled their anxiety. They *had* to win and win consistently if they were to maintain their patriarchal privileges. As a result, they expended a great deal of energy in justifying the losses and would not, perhaps could not, interrogate their motives for keeping Others out and protecting patriarchy. Their justifications deflected attention away from their own gendered privilege and precluded the possibility of a critical analysis of masculinity and power.

The firefighters' discursive strategies – their dogged insistence on justifying the losses – and their lack of critical dialogue worked to stabilize patriarchal power (and the concomitant gendered division of labour in firefighters' workplaces). Their manoeuvres constitute doing gender in the way it is most commonly applied: the reproduction of gender relations of inequality through micro-level interactions. These narratives only temporarily defused the tension created by losing, however, because they did nothing to explain the continued dearth of women and Other men in firefighting. Ignoring obvious inequities does not make them go away. As a result, the crisis continued to simmer beneath the surface, and the turmoil that it spawned often bubbled up in firefighters' talk about their work, suggesting that they continued to grapple with the problem of gender inequality in their organizations.

The New Firefighter

Gender crises, like those fanned by the fire, necessitate a response, a solution to the obvious inconsistencies that threaten the superiority of men. In Connell-speak, crisis tendencies in the gender order require a new answer to the problem of patriarchy (2005). The solution to the tensions created by losing and by the success of female firefighters was a revised configuration of firefighting masculinity. The new firefighter, as discursively constructed by the structural firefighters, was one who distanced himself from the "dumb" blue-collar labourer and aligned himself with a smarter, more technically minded, rational man. The new wildland firefighter disparaged the flamboyance and boorish ignorance of American firefighters and the hypermasculinity of structural firefighters. Both structural and wildland firefighters proudly presented themselves as enlightened, equity aware, and ready to let women in on a level playing field. Both readily acknowledged the skill of their women colleagues (within the confines of a masculine-feminine, male-female binary). These discursive shifts are significant. Nentwich (2008), speaking to the possibilities for gender disruption in heterosexual parenthood, notes that talking the talk is as important as walking the walk: "It seems important not only to engage in alternative practices, but also to *discursively* subvert the heterosexual norm when accounting for or justifying a specific form of parenthood" (211; emphasis added).

The new firefighter is, in some ways, a kinder, gentler version of firefighting masculinity. However, it is also clear that the new firefighter is not ready to give up patriarchal privilege entirely. Revised versions of firefighting masculinities simply provided a provisional answer to the gender crises in firefighters' workplaces without relinquishing patriarchal dividends.

Moreover, this pattern of masculinity remains inherently hierarchical because it is predicated on Othering and difference. The firefighters' discourse was rife with stories that constructed femininity as inadequate and inferior, and they actively used differentiation to exclude Others from their ranks. Furthermore, their gendered strategies of self did not disrupt the gender hierarchy *among men*: the structural firefighters, in tandem with the media, were constructed as heroic exemplars of masculinity, while the firefighters from other groups became failures as workers and as men. Finally, the new firefighter projected the rough edges of working-class, blue-collar masculinity onto Other firefighters in the same way that some middle-class men use the discourse of the new father to thrust rejected dimensions of hegemonic masculinity onto presumably atavistic and sexist racialized men (Hondagneu-Sotelo and Messner 1994).

Firefighting Masculinities and Gender Relations: Connecting the Dots

Earlier I spoke to the importance of theorizing gender as a relational entity. Continuing that thread, it is especially prudent to consider relationality in this case study because the preponderance of empirical evidence speaks most directly to masculinity. For example, there was a good deal of discussion about the firefighters' attempts to distance themselves from other masculinities (such as the "hypermacho"), and femininity and women were analysed only in so far as they enhanced the understanding of masculinity construction. It may appear that I envisage masculinity in isolation, which in turn risks essentializing a fluid social relationship into a static category, an approach I roundly critiqued in chapter 2. As an antidote, I pause to reflect on the ways in which the creating and recreating of masculinities is linked to a system of *gender* relations. Returning to Connell's (1995, 2000a) theoretical framework, masculinities (including the way in which they are constructed in relation to femininity) do not exist in isolation but are patterns of practice that create, and are created by, the social structures of gender relations. These everyday enactments crystallize in firefighters' workplaces, the gender regimes of which are simply institutionalized patterns of gender relations.

The social relations of gender may also be somewhat opaque in this case study because I focused by necessity on men's perceptions of women (that is, Woman as an ideological and cultural representation) and less so on the presence of real, embodied women. Real women certainly inflect the performance of masculinity on the part of men, but the symbolic Woman is also implicated in masculinity construction and, by association, gender relations. To be a masculine man is not to be feminine; hegemonic masculinity is constructed in and through negation of femininity. There is an anti-femininity component of masculinity in which the meaning of being a man is made in constant reference to definitions and representations of femininity. In short, being a man is to be *unlike a Woman*. Likewise for the firefighters, masculinity was created through discussions of what other men were said to be, and was embedded in the disassociation from other masculinities by distancing from femininity (for example, positioning other firefighters as sissies, overly emotional, afraid). Here the connections between the everyday enactment of firefighting masculinities and a broader system of gender inequality became evident.

Remaking Gender

Yet, out of the ashes, the destruction, and the chaos and despite the generally inhospitable environment in firefighting workplaces, the seeds of gender change took root. The work of women firefighters prompted a discursive shift, a new discourse that constituted a modified pattern of gender practice in which women firefighters were praised and supported. These small acts of resistance and accommodation are noteworthy because they take place in the shadow of an occupation that has a long and dubious history of gender and racial exclusivity and a highly masculinized occupational culture. As Thomas and Davis (2005, 729) argue, "micro processes of resistance, although often discounted within a totalizing 'revolution or nothing' conceptualization can still maintain a political project."

So do these practices constitute doing, redoing, or perhaps, even undoing gender? Clearly, sex category continues to matter in the lives of women and men firefighters: they are held accountable to gendered expectations for their particular sex category (West and Zimmerman 2009). This was especially visible in the logical contortions performed by the men firefighters in order to maintain the narrative that firefighting was a man's game, despite their "losing" at that game and freely conceding that women were good at it. On this level their practices constitute doing gender in the reproductive sense.

The crises created by the fire also shook loose some of the tenacious ties that bind sex category to normative expectations for gender practice. Gender was done differently; the boundaries of firefighting masculinity were expanded to include a more egalitarian and flexible discourse by men and some firefighting practices by women. However, the gender binary was not dismantled; gender was redone. Gender, then, can be simultaneously done and redone (Risman 2009). The firefighters both reproduced the gender regimes in their workplaces and destabilized them; their discourse reified gender differences (for example, by situating competent women as gender deviants) and erased them (for example, by claiming that both men and women are genderless). In a similar fashion, as I note above, the new firefighter configuration of masculinity simultaneously reproduces gender inequality and modifies it.

Dichotomous formulations of gender change spawn their own binary; if doing gender is said to create or recreate gender difference, and undoing gender to ameliorate it, one is forced into an either/or model of change. Insisting that actions either do gender or undo gender reifies the very dichotomous thinking against which postmodernists have so emphatically rallied. The firefighters' efforts to grapple with crisis tendencies suggest that a more fruitful theoretical approach to gender change must move beyond a focus on gender difference or similarity to a discussion of the fluidity and complexity of interactions that simultaneously undermine and challenge gender regimes.

These theoretical insights have implications for the field of disaster studies in which gender is generally operationalized through examinations of gender difference. This categorical approach too readily compartmentalizes; it sanitizes the messiness of gender (for example, the possibility that women emergency responders can do or even undo masculinity) and erases the unevenness of gender shifts (for example, disaster events may simultaneously marginalize and benefit some men). Disregarding this incoherence and instability may lead to (1) erroneous conclusions about post-disaster relations of marginalization and hegemony, and (2) obscure spaces in which change can occur or has occurred. The first is important for concerns of social justice, and the second for the broader field of disaster studies, which pays short shrift to instances of and possibilities for progressive change (Nigg and Tierney 1993).

Holding the Line: Crises and the Intransigence of Gender

In the case of the Mountain Park fire, firefighters worked to protect patriarchy, natural resources, and homes but were most successful in their protection of patriarchy. Ultimately, the gender regime of firefighting proved decidedly more fireproof than the houses and trees that so readily succumbed to the flames. The firefighters' discourse reveals that more than twenty years of employment equity legislation and three potentially devastating crises had not completely eliminated male privilege in their workplaces. Why did these crises not undo gender? Why was patriarchy so resilient? How did it retain its force even when its logic was exposed as threadbare?

Masculinities in Crisis

The "doing gender" framework has been criticized for failing to consider the links between the micro and the macro levels, between social interaction and social structure (Moloney and Fenstermaker 2002). In response, West and Zimmerman (2009) stress the mutually constitutive nature of face-to-face interactions and social structures and call for research that advances our understanding of how "historical and structural circumstances bear on the creation and reproduction of social structure in interaction, and how shifts in the former result in changes in the latter" (119).

To understand better the tenacity of gender relations in the wake of the fire, one must examine the connections between macro-level social trends and the firefighters' micro-level gender performances. The gender crises that emerged in the Mountain Park fire did not occur in a vacuum. These tensions coincided with historical shifts in economic, political, and social life that threaten the superiority of privileged men. Contemporary responses to masculinity crises, and the firefighters' active defence of patriarchy, can only be understood in this broader social and historical context. This approach aligns with appeals to de-exceptionalize disasters (Horton 2012) and instead to consider their impacts as extensions of everyday relations of inequality (de Wall 2008).

The Self-Made Man under Siege

With the rise of industrial capitalism, men began to link their gender identities to their position in the marketplace and their achievement of economic success. The proving ground in the public sphere was the workplace, a space in which native-born, white men attempted to demonstrate, prove, and achieve self-made manhood, which was measured by one's accumulated wealth, status, and mobility (Kimmel 1996). Today the workplace, like other traditional spheres of power, is changing in ways that threaten this pattern of masculinity: "The structural foundations of traditional manhood – economic independence, geographic mobility, domestic dominance – have all been eroding. The transformation of the workplace – the decline of the skilled worker, global corporate relocations, the malaise of the middle-class manager, the entry of women into the assembly line and the corporate office – have pressed men to confront their continued reliance on the market-place as the way to demonstrate and prove their manhood" (Kimmel 1996, 299).

Historically, men have used exclusion to reassert masculinity in gender "crises" such as these. According to Kimmel (1996, 101), this strategy was "a conservative reaction against real and perceived threats to increasingly anxious self-made men, as if pushing others out could reassure those who were left that they were, in fact, real men." The non-native-born, homosexuals, women, and racialized Others were used as a screen against which white men projected their fears of emasculation.

The occupation of firefighting has also been a strategic sphere of gender crisis politics, having been called into service in the moments that manhood was thought to be in need of restoration. From the challenges engendered by the emergence of aestheticism and the women's movement in Victorian times (Cooper 1995) to those generated by threats to masculine-coded nationalism in the wake of 11 September 2001 (Malin 2005; Weaver-Hightower 2002), firefighters have provided ready symbols that have been invoked in the service of solidifying and recentring traditional notions of masculinity.

Manhood in the New Economy

In the contemporary labour market most non-credentialled work is found in low-wage-paying service jobs. As such, firefighting is one of an increasingly limited number of desirable occupations for young men who embody a working-class corporeal masculinity based on strength and physical labour (McDowell 2009). Like other blue-collar occupations (for example, the military, police force, trades), it is also one of the last bastions of white, heterosexual, masculine privilege. In the increasingly uncertain world of work this status is threatened. Declining security, wages, and working conditions in many blue-collar jobs (for example see Paap 2006), in addition to pressures for gender equity, mean that defending patriarchal privilege may be perceived as especially urgent by those who feel they are losing ground.

The larger context of instability and change engendered by these historical and contemporary social shifts make the time ripe for the reproduction of a traditional, working man's masculinity based on exclusion and Othering. Those who battled the Mountain Park fire were not immune to the pressures created by these shifts. Like anxious, self-made men, the firefighters attempted to prove their manhood in and through their work and used differentiation to justify barring women from their ranks. That heroes materialized from the ashes further suggests that this model of masculinity was an antidote to cultural anxieties about broader shifts in the gender order. Heroes "embody a culture's most highly prized values" (Lois 2003, 10), and the firefighters provided "proof" that traditional masculinity was alive and well.

Disasters can accelerate trends that are already in progress (Nigg and Tierney 1993), and this is certainly part of the story in the Mountain Park fire. Threats to hegemonic masculinity (real or imagined) invoked efforts to salvage and resurrect it; the firefighters were very much invested in propping up the model of firefighting masculinity that had guaranteed a homogeneous workforce, job security, and living wages in the past. But there was a twist. The events surrounding the disaster, and the gender crises they exacerbated, demanded the production of a new firefighter. The new model and the practices it engendered perceptibly altered the texture of gender relations in firefighters' workplaces. I suspect that the new firefighter would not have had quite the same presence, or even materialized at all, if it had not been for that fateful lightning strike in the remote reaches of Okanagan Mountain Park.

Firefighters' responses to the crises illuminate the connections between broader structural shifts and the ways in which gender was accomplished in and through interactions. These changes, progressive and otherwise, occurred at the micro level in the gender regimes of firefighters' workplaces. So how revolutionary is this reformulated pattern of gender practice, this redoing of gender? What promise does it hold for dismantling gender inequality?

Social movements and shifts in social structures (for example, changes to the legal definition of persons, which enabled women to vote) are well-documented sources of political, cultural, and social change. But micro-level, face-to-face interaction can also spark change – for example, in gender expectations (Deutsch 2007) and discourse (Hollander 2002). Dalton and Fenstermaker (2002) argue that change occurs primarily in the context of interpersonal interactions and their effects on institutional norms: "Some face-to-face interactions ultimately may promote change in the normative standards employed by institutions. When those who violate standards are successful in persuading institutional representatives to subvert institutionally supported practices, they plant the seeds of institutional change. If circumstances and repeated practices allow, actions that were once 'subversive' can later be taken as 'only natural'" (183).

The work of women on the Mountain Park fire was constructed as exemplary (if unusual) by the men working at their side. Praise for women colleagues, including those who did not embody or enact stereotypical femininity, suggests that they were granted more than "conditional acceptance" (Enarson 1984, 144). Women's actions were also noticed by institutional higher-ups (for example, supervisors), whose narratives broke with standard patriarchal institutional discourse. These practices constitute a redoing of gender; sex category continues to matter, and firefighters persist in voicing gender differences, but differently than in the past. This redoing constitutes a shift towards gender equality, as change is often brought about by doing gender differently. Over time, it is plausible that these new practices could lead to broader change through a process of accretion, with the repetition of doing gender differently.

It is also possible that these same men could challenge institutional hiring and promotion practices that perpetuate the gendered division of labour in their organizations. In turn, though once considered "anomalous," the skilled women firefighters could be reconfigured as "normal." This would signal another shift in accountability, one in which gender norms are more inclusive and flexible; multiple configurations of gender practice are celebrated; and, in the best of all possible worlds, an undoing of gender in which one's sex category ceases to matter for the allocation of resources and opportunities. This kind of change is often slow and difficult because the onus is on those who are firmly placed within the boundaries of the institution to help redefine and reframe the normative order (Dalton and Fenstermaker 2002). Yet, in a social milieu with entrenched patterns of social relations, change may only be possible incrementally (Pomerantz, Currie, and Kelly 2004) and through precisely these kinds of everyday resistance.

I surmise that such reconfigurations are especially likely when disasters deepen pre-existing gender cleavages. For example, wildland firefighters – unable to stake a straightforward claim to hegemonic masculinity, and themselves victims of a gender hierarchy based on exclusion and Othering – have far less to gain by defending patriarchy in the event of another crisis. In this case, change may be more desirable and occur more readily in the ranks of wildland firefighting. While theoretically informed, these propositions are necessarily conjectural in

nature. Further research is required before making any definitive conclusions on this front, a point to which I return below.

Continuing to think about change, particularly the absence of change
and the persistence of gender inequalities after the fire, I return to discussing the material dimension of patriarchy that I initiated at the beginning of this case study.

Defending the Social and Material Wages of Firefighting

Symbolic "credibility contests" (Lamont 2000, 179) involving hegemonic
masculinity have implications for the allocation of symbolic and material rewards. Symbolically, men who embody hegemonic masculinity
are given honour, prestige, and authority. Similarly, firefighting masculinity garners "social wages" (Paap 2006, 108) in the form of respect,
honour, recognition, and social status. However, there were also material reasons that the firefighters practised exclusion by laying exclusive
claim to firefighting masculinity. Men who best exemplify hegemonic
masculinity are granted political and material resources. For instance,
men at the top of the social hierarchy earn, on average, higher salaries
than do women (and marginalized men) and are more likely to have political power – resources that can then be used to further their agendas
(Connell 1995). In other words, there are material rewards for those who
win symbolic battles; groups who plausibly assert hegemonic masculinity can use their status to gain power and material resources. There are,
then, important resources at stake in the battle of gender supremacy.
This is a strong incentive for some men to resist change.

In the Mountain Park fire the collective work of the media and the
organization of the firefighting efforts better positioned structural firefighters to stake a socially and culturally valid claim to hegemonic
masculinity. As a result, their gendered strategies of self were more
successful than were those made by other firefighting groups, which
enabled them to translate their symbolic claim to masculinity into material rewards. They literally and figuratively cashed in on their success by converting their collective social capital into a salary increase.
With the help of their union representative, the fire chief, and a media
campaign the structural firefighters successfully rallied the public
and city hall and secured a pay raise, less than one year after the fire.
The firefighters deliberately referred to the fire and their status as heroes to argue that they deserved this salary increase (some firefighters

expressed discomfort with this strategy, but it was used by the group nonetheless).

The fact that the structural firefighters were able to negotiate a higher salary from the very municipality in which hundreds of houses had burned to the ground is a compelling illustration of their victory and power. The City of Kelowna fire chief, who became a local and national celebrity, also reaped significant rewards. He was featured on the cover of a prominent national magazine, received an honorary degree and numerous gifts and awards, was sought for public speaking engagements all over the country, and was asked to run for political office (which he declined).[1]

In the wake of the disaster, the doing and redoing of gender meant that an already privileged group of firefighters continued to receive support and rewards in addition to new material dividends, while the firefighters from other groups were further disenfranchised. The wildland firefighters' organization received some resources, such as more crew positions, but these were jobs that had been cut in recent years and were simply reinstated after the fire.

The issue of who should "rightfully" receive valuable material resources also explains why the firefighters, even when faced with self-admitted failure and the physical presence of skilled women colleagues, did not redefine their gender practices in ways that entirely dispensed with hegemonic masculinity (which would have solved the problem from a logical point of view). Instead they drew on myriad strategies to demonstrate that firefighting is a man's game. Why did they hang on so obstinately to a narrative that was so clearly incoherent? In short, because feminized occupations automatically lose status (Reskin and Roos 1990). If firefighting were perceived as a caring occupation, instead of a paramilitaristic, masculine one, firefighters would likely be paid as well as preschool teachers or nursing home aides. Their strategies speak to the absolute economic necessity of ensuring that everybody understand what masculine characters they are.

Nevertheless, it was not simply that individual stubborn men with quaint or irrational ideas about what it means to be a man prevented a whole-hearted embrace of gender change. Public discourses, reinforced and channelled in large part through the media, were closely tied to the distribution of occupational rewards and supported some patterns of masculinity over others. Partly for this reason, workplace patriarchy is so hard to overcome, even when it is challenged, and gender equity initiatives have made so little progress in changing attitudes. In addition, no matter how clearly illogical are the firefighters' narratives, they "must" be upheld. As Upton Sinclair (1935) so pithily observed over seven decades ago, "it is difficult to get a man to understand something when his salary depends on him not understanding it."

Things can and do change, and we must take the postmodern command to consider fragmentation and disruption seriously. However, "the gender order does not blow away in a breath ... a major reason [is] the persistence of power and wealth, and the active defence of privilege" (Connell 2000a, 14). The social relations between firefighting groups clearly demonstrate the way in which potential challenges to the gender order can be stymied through the protection of hegemonic masculinity in the interests of securing the associated material rewards. This points to the necessity to include material bases of inequality in theories of patriarchy and provides a note of caution for those using discursive gender frameworks in a stand-alone fashion.

The mechanisms by which the privileged defend the material and non-material spoils of patriarchy are also significant for research on gender, disaster, and change. Disasters destroy resources, and those on the margins experience these losses most acutely. At the same time, disasters bring new resources to stricken communities and opportunities for advantaged groups to retain or expand their control of those resources (de Wall 2008; Hearn Morrow and Peacock 1997; Nigg and Tierney 1993). This case study has revealed that one relatively well-placed community group, structural firefighters, secured valuable occupational resources and the gender dynamics behind their "success." Future research could examine the extent to which privileged groups and individuals benefit from the infusion of disaster-related resources and the way in which gender, race, class, and other relations of power are implicated in such cases.

Inching Forward

This study begs the question, Why would privileged groups ever be motivated to facilitate disaster-related change? In the case of the Mountain Park fire, why would firefighters be interested in changing the gender regimes in their workplaces at all, when defending patriarchy seems so rational? The short answer is that only some reap all the benefits of patriarchy, while many more are harmed by this system and the pattern of hegemonic masculinity that supports it. The strategies that firefighters used to attain superior status (that is, gendered strategies of self) and exclude Others from their workplaces do not provide a stable sense of masculinity or empowerment (Barrett 1996; Kimmel 1996). And, ultimately, they further marginalize those who lose the credibility contest.

While the incremental changes in the wake of the Mountain Park fire were restricted to the gender regimes of the firefighters' workplaces, I propose that there are alternative, and perhaps more radical, possibilities for disaster-related change in cases where the uneven distribution of patriarchal benefits is especially pronounced. I refer here to post-disaster settings in which some men receive far fewer benefits than do their more privileged counterparts. These men who are further marginalized are the very men who should, in theory, be invested in change.

Earlier I noted that change is more likely when men's interests are divided, as they were when the social hierarchy developed between firefighting groups. The antagonism between firefighters and the praise for their women colleagues (albeit self-serving) hint at these dynamics. Here I am thinking, though, about more progressive, politically motivated, deeper change and the possibilities for "alliance politics" (Connell 1995, 235; Connell 2005).

As many men have an interest in maintaining gender privilege, they are unlikely to rally around an agenda to eliminate patriarchy. Thus, change is more likely to emerge outside the arena of pure gender politics, in situations where men and women have a common interest in redressing social inequities. The terrains of race relations, labour unions, environmental movements, and anti-colonial struggles are but a few examples of the spaces and moments in which men have collaborated with women to bring about mutually beneficial change. These are also the sites that more clearly illuminate the conflicting interests among different groups of men (Connell 1995; Connell 2005).

Change did not materialize in this way in the aftermath of the Mountain Park fire; the defence of material and symbolic resources, the organizational cultures fixated on winning, the media's investment in heroic masculinity, and the physical location of the fire thwarted transgressive possibilities for gender disruption. Although change was minimal, it would be unwise to throw the proverbial baby out with the bath water. I submit that disasters can generate more progressive change, but it will most likely come from differently situated men.

The firefighters who battled the Mountain Park fire are a relatively fortunate group; hence, their claim to hegemonic masculinity (while not without its difficulties) is more socially legitimate than claims that others can assert. Men marginalized by race, ethnicity, class, sexuality, and citizenship or nation must work far more strenuously to prove masculinity, a task that is nearly impossible in the case of highly regarded configurations like hegemonic masculinity. Marginalized men are not granted the same licence or permitted the same freedom to fall short in their practice. Presumed to be gender failures, they must convincingly demonstrate otherwise. As such, their masculinity performances are not socially sanctioned in the same way as are those of privileged men.

These gender dynamics create possibilities for political alliances with women in the wake of disasters. Men who cannot so readily declare or practise hegemonic masculinity must, by choice or circumstance, configure gender differently. When these men face disaster-related inequities, they are further marginalized and, hence, have much to gain in altering the status quo. In theory, these men will be especially motivated to form political solidarities with similarly disenfranchised Others (including women). Here it is possible to imagine coalitions forming around social inequalities in housing and relocation, resource distribution, insurance settlements, environmental hazards, or human rights violations. The struggles for social justice may also include, and in some cases necessitate, a redoing or even undoing of gender. As gender relations intersect with multiple modalities of power (Hill Collins 2000), progressive shifts in one domain may ripple into connected domains.

As change is often uneven, it would be naive to propose that men and women on the peripheries will spontaneously band together in the aftermath of disaster to create progressive change. Coalitions of this sort first require the recognition of men as potential comrades in struggle, and a concerted effort by men and women invested in issues of social justice, to make that happen. Although the possibility of gendered power relationships may exist in alliance politics, this should not prevent acknowledgment of the potential for progressive change through coalitions with marginal men.

My claim that men who are disenfranchised by disaster will be likelier to reconfigure gender and engage in alliance politics is theoretical. Disasters can create occasions for new groups and organizations to emerge and for alliances to form among disenfranchised groups, even for those without a history of political activism (Hearn Morrow and Peacock 1997), but only further empirical research can illuminate the way in which these factions articulate with gender relations. Towards this end, future work should consider the experiences of marginalized men, to wit, how masculinities are shaped in response to injustices occasioned by disasters, including the formation of strategic coalitions with others on the fringes of social hierarchies. This research could explore more deeply than I have done here the ways in which gender intersects with other structures of inequality such as race, ethnicity, and nation, and the implications that this has for the politics of post-disaster change. Finally, where feasible, longitudinal methods could be employed to illuminate both short-term disruptions and stabler, enduring shifts.

Social scientists, policymakers, and others concerned with issues of social justice have much to learn about social inequalities and the potential for change generated by disasters. These are issues of pressing concern in an increasingly polarized socio-political global order that is haunted by the spectre of ever more catastrophic disasters. Those on the margins are certain to suffer most deeply from the landscapes of despair borne by these events, but it may also be by virtue of social dispossession that the impetus for change is forged – a process writ large in recent political uprisings such as Idle No More, the global Occupy movement, and the Arab Spring. Disaster social scientists have a key role to play in researching and documenting change from the peripheries in all of its complexity and discovering how it can inform the efforts to mitigate inequities – perhaps even contributing along the way to the transformation of "global citizenship" from a fashionable leitmotif to the practice of meaningful social action.

Appendix:
Dilemmas, Tensions, and Contradictions in Feminist-Inspired Research*

The "crisis of representation" (Denzin and Lincoln 2000, 3) that has been spawned by postmodern critique has raised questions such as, who can or should speak for whom? and how should research participants' lives and experiences be presented or re-presented in social science research and writing? Feminists have likewise been attentive to issues of power and persist in illuminating the "micropolitics" (Bhavnani 1993, 98) of social research, acknowledging, for instance, that researchers have the most and often final authority over the form and content of the written text. A fundamental tenet of feminist research, therefore, is to minimize the power differences between researchers and participants (Harding and Norberg 2005; Naples 2003).

Towards this end, feminist social scientists have developed interview principles that aim to diminish these power differentials. For instance, researchers are instructed to become equals in a dialogic exchange with participants (Fontana 2001) and to establish empathy and rapport with those whom they interview (Luff 1999; Taylor 1998). Much of this feminist writing is directed at women who are doing interviews with and for women (Finch 1993; Oakley 1981). The assumption is usually that the interviewer has more power than has the interviewee, and discussions are often about white, middle-class academic women interviewing marginalized women (for example see Armstead 1995).[1] Furthermore, feminist researchers have long focused on women's experiences and placed

*Excerpted by permission of the publishers from "Interviewing Elite Men: Feminist Reflections on Studying 'Up' and Selling Out," in *Researching amongst Elites*, ed. Luis L.M. Aguiar and Christopher J. Schneider (Farnham, UK: Ashgate, 2012), 199–215.

them at the centre of analysis, with the political goal of making visible the social locations and knowledge of such marginalized women.[2]

Recent theoretical developments have complicated the notion of an up-down power binary between researchers and participants, and "the image of the powerless respondent has altered with the recognition that researchers' 'power' is often only partial and tenuous" (Olesen 2000, 234) and that participants can and do exercise power in the production of the research product (Thapar-Björkert and Henry 2004). These insights echo broader theoretical approaches which maintain that power is not static but fluid, multi-directional, contextual, and negotiated (Campbell 2003; Foucault 1980).

Dilemmas of a Feminist Researcher

The aforementioned texts informed my methodological approach in this case study and raised a number of questions to which I had no clear answers. Troubling the notion of an up-down power dichotomy meant that simply by virtue of my researcher status I would not wield more power than would my participants, but it did not make sense to assume that my interviewees would be all-powerful. The fact that most participants were relatively privileged men added another layer of complexity.

Interviews with Men

Over two decades ago, scholars such as Sandra Harding (1987) defined the field of feminist methodology as one that centres women's experiences and produces research for women. In the years that followed, the ethics of interviewing women were subsequently widely discussed and documented (for example see Finch 1993 and Oakley 1981). The inclusion of men, however, brings new issues to bear on feminist-inspired interviewing practices. In particular, I wondered how to practise feminist research principles based on democracy and transparency in interviews with men who had a history of resistance to gender equality. How could I, as a feminist researcher, interview a community of privileged men without resorting to essentialist notions of gender or categorical notions of power? In the end, could I perform feminist research with this group of men or would it mean selling out as a feminist?

I wanted to employ feminist interview principles in my work with firefighters not only because I am a committed feminist, but because those principles held the promise of creating quality data by mitigating threats to participants' enactment of gender. However, they did not map neatly onto my research project. I could not ignore the fact that my participants were mostly privileged men, a group with a history of resistance to infiltration by outsiders and one that garnered respect and prestige in the community. And, as a feminist, I could not overlook the fact that, on many levels, these men benefited from gender inequality.

At the same time, I did not want to prematurely conclude that firefighters were anti-feminist simply because they were men. Women may also be resistant to feminist research (for example see Luff 1999), and intersectional theorizing has seriously undermined the notion of essential differences between women and men. I had to recognize the complexity in the social locations and subjectivities of the men in my study.

Finally, postmodern troubling of an up-down power binary and the notion that power flows in a top-down fashion meant that it was problematic to presume that men firefighters were more powerful than I was, or vice versa. So my challenge was to avoid automatically privileging gender as an analytic lens (Rice 2009), while simultaneously recognizing the privileges enjoyed by men firefighters as a group.

Disclosure, Reciprocity, and Rapport

Inspired by the early work of Anne Oakley (1981), feminist researchers championed reciprocity, self-disclosure, and rapport as a way to minimize the power differences between women interviewers and participants (for example see Hertz 1995 and Taylor 1998), the former thought to have more power than the latter. The stated goals were to develop more egalitarian and reciprocal relationships with interviewees (for example, the interviewer shifts from being a neutral questioner to being a participant, while participants are given the freedom to ask questions of the interviewer); to allow women to describe their experiences in their own terms; and to encourage research participants to introduce new questions based on their own lived experiences (Hertz 1995; Taylor 1998).

These principles have now been contested. For example, efforts to diminish power differences between women have been critiqued by those who argue that these manoeuvres overlook the political issues around knowledge production and consumption (for example see McCorkel and Myers 2003 and Rice 2009). Equally problematic for my study was the fact that these discussions had not been extended to include research with men, which left me with few guidelines for my interviews. It seemed problematic to apply feminist principles of reciprocity, disclosure, and rapport to a study of privileged men, but, at the same time, if power is non-linear and fluid, disclosure, reciprocity, and rapport between myself and my participants was, at the very least, a possibility.

Moreover, the application of these guidelines was not only possible but potentially necessary for obtaining quality data when interviewing men. Here my thoughts were informed by the work of Schwalbe and Wolkomir (2002) who note that masculinity dynamics are embedded in the interview process: "[The interview is] an opportunity to signify masculinity inasmuch as men are allowed to portray themselves as in control, autonomous, rational, and so on. It is a threat inasmuch as an interviewer controls the interaction, asks questions that put these elements of manly self-portrayal into doubt, and does not simply affirm a man's masculinity displays" (205–6). The interviewer has control in that she sets the agenda, asks the questions, and probes for information. Participants relinquish some control over the process, and they also risk having their public self discredited. When respondents' masculinity is threatened, they may employ a number of strategies in an attempt to save face, such as trying to control the interview situation, limiting disclosure of emotions, and exaggerating rationality, autonomy, and control. The researcher's job, therefore, is to employ questioning and probing strategies that reduce this threat to participants' masculine selves (Schwalbe and Wolkomir 2002).

It seemed reasonable to expect that masculinity would be especially salient in my interviews with firefighters, not only because firefighting is a highly masculinized occupation but because the firefighters were on the defensive owing to the unprecedented losses caused by the wildfire. Furthermore, because they have a long history of excluding outsiders, it was plausible that at least some participants would try to control the flow, the content, and even the dissemination of the information.

Since I wanted to obtain quality data and, where possible, draw on feminist research principles, I was motivated to pay close attention to the power dynamics in the interviews and to attempt to minimize the threats to participants' masculinity. Heralded as tools for mitigating power dynamics, the principles of disclosure, reciprocity, and rapport had the potential to serve double duty as mechanisms for reducing threats to masculinity in the interviews. In what follows I discuss the way in which I worked to put them into practice, and some of the dilemmas I faced along the way.

Disclosure and the Undercover Feminist

In the interests of transparency and reflexivity many feminists call for disclosure of their identities in order to place themselves on the same "critical plane" as are the participants (Bloom, quoted in Rice 2009, 249). This is a laudable strategy when used by researchers to interrogate their own social locations and the ways in which they are implicated in their research, as Rice (2009) does so eloquently in her study of women's embodiment.

When self-disclosure entails sharing personal information with participants, it is more likely to have the intended effect if the researchers share a particular world view or experience with their participants. I could not assume, however, that this was the case in my research with firefighters. I was entering what was very likely a "politically resistant community" (Klatch 1988, 74). Since firefighters reap rewards through exclusion, it was not unreasonable to expect that they would be resistant to a feminist political agenda of inclusion and social change. Furthermore, Schwalbe and Wolkomir (2002) counsel that masculinity threats are heightened when participants are aware that the interviewer is interested in gender. As a result, I felt that revealing myself as a feminist researcher interested in gender relations and political change would be risky at best (if it had negative repercussions for rapport with participants) and academically disastrous at worst (if organizational gatekeepers chose to freeze me out).

The possibility of entering the field as a covert feminist also raised the thorny issue of informed consent. Researchers are mandated to provide potential participants with sufficient information to make educated decisions about participating. Seemingly straightforward, informed consent presents a number of challenges, one being whether or not critical researchers are obligated to disclose all the details of their research to powerful groups (who, for obvious reasons, may decline to participate if they are made aware that they will be critically evaluated). Thorne (2004) suggests that elite groups are less in need of the protections granted by the principles of informed consent. While this may make sense in theory, it is troublesome given the feminist research principle of self-disclosure. In the end, I chose, like others before me (for example see Arendell 1997), not to disclose my feminist status unless I was asked directly, which I never was. I did, however, make my interest in gender known in the synopsis of the research results that I gave to interested participants at the conclusion of the study.

Being an undercover feminist created a number of additional dilemmas. Many firefighters agreed to assist me with my research, were generous with their time, and had little to gain from doing so. As a result I felt indebted to them. And while I did not necessarily agree with the firefighters' politics, it did not preclude me from appreciating their views on various topics. In fact, I liked many of the people whom I met; some firefighters were funny, some were sincere, and most were thoughtful. All of this made me uncomfortable about concealing my feminist identity. My covert status also restricted the degree to which I could reciprocate by disclosing my thoughts and feelings, both during interviews and in interactions outside of the interviews. This caused some guilt because I had hoped that participants would share with me the very depth of information, feeling, and emotion that I was withholding from them.

When I did engage in self-disclosure, it was not necessarily in an attempt to alter power dynamics. Instead, I often revealed personal information when I thought it would help me to gain access to a site, a participant, or important information. Some aspects of my personal history (that I had experienced a natural disaster and had grown up in the area) positioned me as an ally, and I shared this information when selling my project to gatekeepers, when soliciting participants, and when commiserating with firefighters on issues of mutual concern. On some levels my strategies were entirely self-serving and, one might argue, counter to feminist research mandates to minimize power differences (an issue to which I return below).

Reciprocity, Power, and Control

Reciprocity may include, but is not limited to, sharing knowledge and experiences with participants (Cotterill 1992), becoming friends (Oakley 1981), and granting participants some control over the interview process (Campbell 2003). Given the threat to masculinity that could be engendered by the interview method, I focused on the third strategy and gave firefighters opportunities to shape the format, content, time, and location of their interviews.

I wanted the firefighters to respond thoughtfully to my questions, so I reciprocated by listening to them speak about issues that they felt were important, even when those issues seemed to be tangential to the project. When I sensed that participants wanted to air an issue, I listened attentively until they had finished and commiserated when appropriate by saying, "I can see why you'd be upset about that." I also gave interviewees some control over the way in which the interview unfolded. For example, I did not prevent participants from deviating from the topic at hand; instead, I circled back to my question after they had had a chance to speak. In several cases, the firefighters' lengthy diatribes created time constraints, and I was unable to ask some questions. Finally, I gave each participant a chance to add comments near the end of the interview.

Unfortunately, in some cases my efforts backfired when firefighters used these opportunities for reciprocity to assert their agency in ways that affronted my feminist sensibilities and, in one case, compromised the quality of the interview.[3] On this occasion an administrator in the structural fire department directed his entire interview, dictated which topics were covered, took a phone call while I waited, checked the clock several times, and, when the allotted time was up, asked, "Do you have enough?" effectively announcing that he was ready to end our conversation. More commonly, though, I was interrupted while asking questions or making comments during interviews (younger wildland firefighters were much less likely to do so). In another instance, a structural firefighter whom I interviewed while doing a driving tour of burned neighbourhoods provided numerous unsolicited driving tips. In the end, I worried that sharing control of the manner in which the interviews unfolded and the conditions under which they took place reinforced norms of gendered interaction in which women are empathetic listeners and facilitators of men's narratives (Pini 2005).

Interpretive Rapport

Another rationale for not revealing my feminist identity and research agenda was that I believed it would hinder the rapport with participants. Rapport is important for obtaining quality data. However, it is important to distinguish between a manipulative rapport that objectifies participants by attempting to exercise control over them in order to "extract" data, and an "interpretive rapport" that aims to foster mutual understanding (Campbell 2003, 290).

I strove to employ an interpretive rapport, but on more than one occasion I experienced much personal discomfort. For example, I sometimes agreed with sexist remarks even though I found them to be highly offensive. Usually my agreement was implicit; I simply did not say anything in response to these comments. A number of times it was more explicit, for example by nodding my head or laughing. On two separate occasions I did not challenge men who made homophobic remarks. For example, one structural firefighter, talking about a medical training program, belittled a gay classmate by implying that he was "half" a man.

On the one hand, I was upset that I was complicit in homophobic and overtly sexist constructions of gender. I wondered if my passivity simply reified negative stereotypes about women and gay men. On the other hand, I wanted to understand firefighters' worlds and world views, and had I challenged them, it would have been because I wanted to try to *change* their views. In addition, I had another motive: I needed their cooperation, and I was concerned that objections to their comments could undermine their masculinity performance and compromise the interview process. Similar to Glebbeek's dilemma in her interviews with police (Huggins and Glebbeek 2003), I garnered cooperation by disregarding participants' offensive comments. I found some comfort in deciding to save my critical analysis for the written products (Arendell 1997), but in the end I felt as though I were selling out as a feminist on two fronts: (i) for not challenging firefighters' sexism and homophobia and (ii) for using rapport-building strategies in an objectifying way. This dilemma was further complicated because I was sympathetic to some of the fire-related concerns expressed by the firefighters, and I could not help but feel compassion for those who cried or struggled to hold back tears in the interviews.

Campbell's (2003) notion of critical dialogue is partially instructive here. She argues that "dialogue suggests connection without requiring empathy and acceptance of all that is said, and when qualified by 'critical,' [it] allows for challenge" (293). In my interviews with firefighters I hoped to create dialogue even though I did not agree with everything that they said, but I did not employ Campbell's critical interview style, because I did not confront firefighters when faced with sexist or homophobic remarks.

THE PARTICIPANT AS EXPERT

Another technique used in an effort to establish interpretive rapport was the positioning of participants as experts. I highlighted that I was largely uninformed about the occupation of firefighting, because I wanted participants to know that they had expert knowledge that I did not have and therefore I needed their assistance to understand it. This positioned the interviewee as the authority and me as the "student" (Hoffman 2007, 323) who was interested in learning more about the occupation of firefighting. This strategy seemed especially important given my status as an academic; always conscious of potential threats to masculinity, I did not want the firefighters to feel intimidated by my post-secondary education. Ultimately, asking firefighters to explain various dimensions of their jobs also meant sharing control. Moreover, encouraging them to share their knowledge worked to develop a mutual understanding of the sort that fosters interpretive rapport.

On the downside, my attempts to make the interviews non-threatening created an ethical dilemma. When I invoked the naive researcher role in order to position participants as experts, it very likely reinforced the stereotypes of women as largely incompetent and uneducated about "men's work." This strategy also felt overly manipulative in the last few interviews because by then I had accumulated a solid base of knowledge on firefighting and was no longer the uninformed researcher that I purported to be.

Destabilizing Binaries: Power and the Dialectic of Control

When I began interviewing firefighters, it was clear that the power dynamics were not straightforward. I certainly had some degree of control over the research process by virtue of my status as a middle-class academic, one with the ability to present or re-present participants' narratives in ways that I deemed appropriate. It was also apparent that my participants were privileged on some dimensions; they had the ability to freeze me out, to speak disrespectfully about outsiders without fear of reprisal, to dictate the location and timing of the interviews, and to share in directing the flow and content of those interviews. This was, of course, partly owing to my efforts to reduce the potential threats to firefighters' masculinities. It was not surprising, therefore, that I did not feel all powerful in the interviews. Rather, I sensed an implicit (and sometimes overt) jockeying for control.

Minimizing threat might be viewed as a way to democratize the research process in the sense that the goal is to share power in order not to undermine the "doing" of masculinity. However, it can be unjust (and inconsistent with feminist research ethics) when it results in an objectifying rapport, one in which researchers are instructed to manipulate the interview dynamics in ways that reduce masculinity threats because such threats are thought to interfere with the extraction of quality data (for example, participants may resist showing emotion).

Having now had the luxury of reflection, I recognize that to view my navigation of masculinity dynamics as anti-democratic is to miss the postmodern point that power is multi-directional, shifting, and contextual. If this is indeed the case, research practices cannot be classified as either hierarchical or anti-hierarchical. Campbell (2003, 299–300) discusses the limitations of describing the power dynamics of interviewing in such categorical terms:

> Power in and over the research process is not concentrated in the hands of either the research or the researched. This does not amount to "power sharing" or "democracy," which implies some sort of mutual recognition about the epistemological, methodological and analytical routes that are taken, but is part of a "power struggle" – a dialectic of control ... perfectly captures the dynamic nature of the interviewing process and its embeddedness within a wider configuration of power relations; it prises open the straitjacket of the hierarchy/democracy dyad and exposes the complexity of the interactive exercise of power; it offers a new slant on old debates about gender, race and/or class relations of interviewing; and it avoids preconceptions about who controls the interviewing process, how control is achieved, and to what effect.

Some of my strategies certainly privileged *my* needs and interests. At the same time, the firefighters had some control over the interviews and the ability to block access to their closed group. The interviews, therefore, were more accurately characterized by a dialectic of control in which the participants and I engaged in struggles over setting the terms of access and defining the contours of the interviews.

The dialectic of control is also consistent with a formulation of power as a shifting social relationship, rather than an intrinsic, stable, individual possession that one either has or does not have. As Hannah Arendt (1958, 200) explains, "power is always, as we would say, a power potential and not an unchangeable, measurable, and reliable entity like force or strength. While strength is the natural quality of an individual seen in isolation, power springs up between men when they act together and vanishes the moment they disperse." An understanding of power as flowing in and through social life directs attention away from questions about who has more, or less, power – the researchers or the participants – to questions about the extent to which researchers and participants can exercise agency in the context of the shifting power relationships in which they are embedded.

Had I concluded this earlier in my study, I would have been less concerned about minimizing threats to masculinity, because this approach reflects a binary model of power based on the assumption that interviewers have more power than do interviewees (who are thus threatened when they must relinquish the power and control that they are thought to have in all other situations). The jockeying for control that characterized my interviews was indicative of a dialectic of control, and it calls into question the validity of the binary model. Specifically, the formulation of power on which a dialectic of control is premised means that feminist research principles cannot be applied in an either/or fashion in work with men.

Conceptualizing interview dynamics as dialectic in nature also opens a space for the kind of critical dialogue championed by Campbell (2003). As noted earlier, while I aimed to understand firefighters' world views through mutual dialogue, I did not implement the critical dimension of this formulation. Had I been prepared for the extent to which firefighters asserted their agency, I would have further interrogated the suggestion that interviewers must reduce threats to masculinity in order to obtain quality data. Instead of attempting to minimize these at all costs by affirming firefighters' masculinity displays, I would have more readily engaged them in dialogue about homophobic and sexist comments. In turn, this could have further illuminated firefighters' world views. And, in the end, perhaps I would not have had the nagging feeling that I had sold out as a feminist.

Notes

1 Environment Canada ranks tornado severity on a Fujita scale of one to five according to damage caused. Rank four is classified as "devastating" (Environment Canada 2010).

1. Black Fridays

1 All names are pseudonyms, and some participants have multiple pseudonyms in order to protect their identity.
2 From this point forward, I refer to the fire as the Mountain Park fire.
3 One hectare is the equivalent of 2.471 acres.
4 Fuel is the combustible material needed for a wildfire to burn, such as trees, brush, and other vegetation. The more fuel available in a wildfire, the more difficult it is to put out the fire (Filmon 2004).
5 About 4.2 million hectares of forest were attacked by the Mountain Pine Beetle in 2002 (BC Ministry of Forests and Range 2010).
6 The wildland-urban interface is the geographical point at which wilderness and urban development meet. In an interface fire, structures and vegetation are sufficiently close that a wildfire spreads to structures, and/or a structural fire ignites trees and vegetation (BC Ministry of Forests, Protection Branch 2004a).
7 The information in this section was obtained from interviews and the "Fire Review Summary for the Okanagan Mountain Park Fire" (BC Ministry of Forests, Protection Branch 2003).
8 The Ministry of Forests Protection Branch (2006d) utilizes a fire-intensity ranking system ranging from rank 1 (a smouldering fire with no open

flames) to rank 6 (blow-up or conflagration; violent fire behaviour with a rate of spread in excess of 18 metres per minute).

2. Methodological and Theoretical Road Map

1 Fireguards separate the fuel from the fire, thereby halting or slowing the fire's advance. This involves cutting, scraping, or digging a swath of ground clear of all combustible materials.

2 Hereafter, the Ministry of Forests and Range will be called the Ministry of Forests.

3 Most of the firefighters appeared to identify as heterosexual, as many mentioned wives or girlfriends in the interviews. However, sexuality is often invisible (especially in homophobic environments), so I cannot say with certainty that all of the firefighters would identify themselves as heterosexual.

4 See Fothergill (1998) for a thorough review of the literature.

5 For exceptions see Alway, Liska Belgrave, Smith (1998), Klinenberg (2003), Luft (2008), and Palinkas, Downs, Petterson, Russell (1993).

6 For a thorough review of these debates see Walby (1989) and Young (2005).

3. Firefighting Is a Man's Game

1 Statistics Canada draws on the Employment Equity Act, which defines *visible minorities* as "persons, other than Aboriginal peoples, who are non-Caucasian in race or non-white in colour." As a result, these percentages do not include Aboriginal peoples.

2 There was one woman firefighter working at the Kelowna airport at the time of the study.

3 Mark's American counterparts also are fond of saying, "We run into burning buildings while other people are running out" (Chetkovich 1997).

4 In a similar vein, Britton (1997) found that men corrections officers relied on the relatively remote possibility of inmate violence in order to frame resistance to women working in men's prisons. Interestingly, structural firefighters are spending less and less time actually fighting fires (Childs, Morris, Ingham 2004) owing to improved safety standards such as smoke detectors and stricter building codes. So the argument that firefighters must be strong enough to drag a person out of a burning building as justification for excluding women is not as convincing as it once might have been.

5 In addition to differentiation, there were other mechanisms that functioned to exclude women firefighters or, at the very least, keep their numbers low,

such as hiring practices that relied on social networks (in both structural and wildland firefighting organizations).

4. "We Felt Like We Lost"

1 Kris Paap (2006) makes a similar argument in the context of construction work.
2 Two interface fires occurred on the west side of Okanagan Lake in the summer of 2009. They were fought by wildland firefighters and structural firefighters from the district of West Kelowna. Three homes burned to the ground, and a large sawmill narrowly escaped the flames.

5. Navigating Hierarchy and Contesting Masculinities

1 As I noted earlier, there was one incident in which a wildland firefighter publicly criticized the structural fire department, but the story was quickly quashed and an apology issued. In addition, the structural fire department was sued by several insurance companies, suggesting that the insurers believed the firefighters to be negligent. Overall, however, non-structural firefighters were subjected to far greater criticism.

6. Working with the Other

1 Protective pants worn when one is working with a chain saw.
2 Similarly, the wildland firefighters studied by Desmond (2007) viewed their female colleagues as anomalies.

7. Out of the Ashes

1 Even after retiring from the fire service, the chief continued to garner significant public support. For example, in 2009 he fell critically ill, and a prayer service drew thousands of supporters, including the premier of British Columbia. Two years later he won a seat on Kelowna City Council.

Appendix

1 For an exception see Ross (2001).
2 For a thorough review of feminist research paradigms and methods see Olesen (2000).
3 In a similar vein, Thapar-Bjorkert and Henry (2004) found that some of their participants used reciprocity to create spaces in which they could exercise power.

References

Acker, Joan. 1990. "Hierarchies, Jobs, Bodies: A Theory of Gendered Organizations." *Gender & Society* 4 (2): 139–58. http://dx.doi.org/10.1177/089124390004002002.

Altheide, D. 2001. *Creating Fear: News and the Construction of Crisis*. New York: Aldine De Gruyter.

Alway, Joan, Linda Liska Belgrave, and Kenneth J. Smith. 1998. "Back to Normal: Gender and Disaster." *Symbolic Interaction* 21 (2): 175–95. http://dx.doi.org/10.1525/si.1998.21.2.175.

Andersen, Margaret L. 2005. "Thinking About Women: A Quarter Century's View." *Gender & Society* 19 (4): 437–55. http://dx.doi.org/10.1177/0891243205276756.

Arendell, Terry. 1997. "Reflections on the Researcher-Researched Relationship: A Woman Interviewing Men." *Qualitative Sociology* 20 (3): 341–68. http://dx.doi.org/10.1023/A:1024727316052.

Arendt, Hannah. 1958. *The Human Condition*. Chicago: University of Chicago Press.

Armstead, Cathleen. 1995. "Writing Contradictions: Feminist Research and Feminist Writing." *Women's Studies International Forum* 18 (5-6): 627–36. http://dx.doi.org/10.1016/0277-5395(95)00084-4.

Bari, F. 1998. "Gender, Disaster, and Empowerment: A Case Study from Pakistan." In *The Gendered Terrain of Disaster: Through Women's Eyes*, ed. E. Enarson and B. Hearn Morrow, 125–31. Westport, CT: Praeger.

Barrett, Frank. 1996. "The Organizational Construction of Hegemonic Masculinity: The Case of the US Navy." *Gender, Work and Organization* 3 (3): 129–42. http://dx.doi.org/10.1111/j.1468-0432.1996.tb00054.x.

BC Ministry of Forests and Range. 2010. "Mountain Pine Beetle in B.C." Retrieved 1 July 2010 (http://www.for.gov.bc.ca/hfp/mountain_pine_beetle/bbbrochure.htm).

BC Ministry of Forests, Protection Branch. 2003. "Fire Review Summary for Okanagan Mountain Fire." Retrieved 20 January 2004 (http://www.for.gov.bc.ca/protect/reports/2003review/okanagan%5Ffire%5Freview%5Fk50628.pdf).

BC Ministry of Forests, Protection Branch. 2004a. "Interface Fires and Safety." Retrieved 1 October 2004 (http://www.for.gov.bc.ca/protect/FAQ/interface.htm#32).

BC Ministry of Forests, Protection Branch. 2004b. "Wildfire News." Retrieved 22 April 2004 (http://www.for.gov.bc.ca/pScripts/Protect/WildfireNews/index.asp?Page=Project&ID=9).

BC Ministry of Forests, Protection Branch. 2006a. "2000 Recap." Retrieved 24 March 2006 (http://www.for.gov.bc.ca/protect/reports/FireSeasonReview.htm).

BC Ministry of Forests, Protection Branch. 2006b. "Causes of Fires." Retrieved 29 March 2006 (http://www.for.gov.bc.ca/protect/FAQ/causes.htm#22).

BC Ministry of Forests, Protection Branch. 2006c. "Fire Management Teams." Retrieved 15 March 2006 (http://www.for.gov.bc.ca/protect/suppression/imt.htm).

BC Ministry of Forests, Protection Branch. 2006d. "Fire Rank." Retrieved 22 March 2006 (http://www.for.gov.bc.ca/protect/suppression/FireRank.htm).

BC Ministry of Forests, Protection Branch. 2006e. "Fire Review Summary for Okanagan Mountain Fire." Retrieved 24 March 2006 (http://www.for.gov.bc.ca/protect/reports/2003review/okanagan_fire_review_k50628.pdf).

BC Ministry of Forests, Protection Branch. 2006f. "Types of Fire Crews." Retrieved 28 March 2006 (http://www.for.gov.bc.ca/protect/crews/).

BC Ministry of Forests, Protection Branch. 2006g. "Air Tankers." Retrieved 27 March 2006 (http://www.for.gov.bc.ca/protect/aviation/airtankers.htm).

BC Ministry of Forests, Protection Branch. 2006h "Kamloops Fire Center." Retrieved 27 March 2006 (http://www.for.gov.bc.ca/protect/organization/kamloops/index.htm).

BC Ministry of Forests, Protection Branch. 2006i. "Prescribed Fire." Retrieved 27 March 2006 (http://www.for.gov.bc.ca/protect/burning/prescribedfire.htm#nature).

BC Ministry of Forests, Protection Branch. 2006j. "Protection Branch: Average Hectares, Fires, and Dollars." Retrieved 27 March 2006 (http://www.for.gov.bc.ca/protect/reports/HistoricalAverages.htm).

BC Ministry of Forests, Wildfire Management Branch. 2010a. "About Us." Retrieved 18 October 2010 (http://bcwildfire.ca/AboutUs/).

BC Ministry of Forests, Wildfire Management Branch. 2010b. "Employment: Frequently Asked Questions." Retrieved 14 September 2010 (http://bcwildfire.ca/employment/firefighter/faq.htm).

BC Ministry of Forests, Wildfire Management Branch. 2010c. "Prescribed Fire." Retrieved 19 October 2010 (http://bcwildfire.ca/Prevention/PrescribedFire/).

BC Ministry of Forests, Wildfire Management Branch. 2011. "Firefighters and Staff FAQ." Retrieved 25 August 2011 (http://bcwildfire.ca/FAQ/staff.htm#17).

Beck, U. 2006. "Living in the World Risk Society." *Economy and Society* 35 (3): 329–45. http://dx.doi.org/10.1080/03085140600844902.

Beechey, Veronica. 1979. "On Patriarchy." *Feminist Review* 3 (1): 66–82. http://dx.doi.org/10.1057/fr.1979.21.

Berg, Bruce L. 2001. *Qualitative Research Methods for the Social Sciences*. Needham Heights, MA: Allyn and Bacon.

Bhavnani, K.K. 1993. "Tracing the Contours: Feminist Research and Feminist Objectivity." *Women's Studies International Forum* 16 (2): 95–104. http://dx.doi.org/10.1016/0277-5395(93)90001-P.

Bird, Sharon. 1996. "Welcome to the Men's Club: Homosociality and the Maintenance of Hegemonic Masculinity." *Gender & Society* 10 (2): 120–32. http://dx.doi.org/10.1177/089124396010002002.

Bourdieu, Pierre. 1984. *Distinction: A Social Critique of the Judgement of Taste*. Cambridge, MA: Harvard University Press.

Bourdieu, Pierre. 1986. "The Forms of Capital." In *Handbook of Theory and Research for the Sociology of Education*, ed. J. Richardson, 241–58. New York: Greenwood.

Bourdieu, Pierre. 1990. *The Logic of Practice*. Stanford, CA: Stanford University Press.

Bradshaw, Sarah. 2001. "Reconstructing Roles and Relations: Women's Participation in Reconstruction in Post-Mitch Nicaragua." *Gender and Development* 9 (3): 79–87. http://dx.doi.org/10.1080/13552070127757.

Bradshaw, Sarah, and Brian Linneker. 2009. "Gender Perspectives on Disaster Reconstruction in Nicaragua: Reconstructing Roles and Relations?" In *Women, Gender and Disaster: Global Issues and Initiatives*, ed. E. Enarson and P.G.D. Chakrabarti, 75–88. Thousand Oaks, CA: Sage.

Brannon, R. 1976. "The Male Sex Role – And What It's Done for Us Lately." In *The Forty-Nine Percent Majority*, ed. R. Brannon and D. David, 1–40. Reading, MA: Addison-Wesley.

Briceno, Salvano. 2009. Foreword. In *Women, Gender and Disaster: Global Issues and Initiatives*, ed. E. Enarson and P.G. Dhar Chakrabarti, p. xiii. Thousand Oaks, CA: Sage.

Britton, Dana. 1997. "Gendered Organizational Logic: Policy and Practice in Men's and Women's Prisons." *Gender & Society* 11 (6): 796–818. http://dx.doi.org/10.1177/089124397011006005.

Britton, Dana. 2003. *At Work in the Iron Cage: The Prison as a Gendered Organization.* New York: New York University Press.

Brunsma, D.L., D. Overfelt, and J.S. Picou. 2007. *The Sociology of Katrina: Perspectives on a Modern Catastrophe.* Rowman & Littlefield.

Butler, Judith. 2004. *Undoing Gender.* New York: Routledge.

Butterfield, Alicia. 2009. "Gender in Crisis: An Anthropological Perspective on Internally Displaced Persons and Humanitarian Initiatives in Sri Lanka." Anthropology, San Diego State University, San Diego.

Button, Gregory, and Anthony Oliver-Smith. 2008. "Disaster, Displacement, and Employment: Distortion of Labor Markets during Post-Katrina Reconstruction." In *Capitalizing on Catastrophe*, ed. N. Gunewardena and M. Schuller, 123–45. Lanham, MD: Altamira Press.

Campbell, Elaine. 2003. "Interviewing Men in Uniform: A Feminist Approach?" *International Journal of Social Research Methodology* 6 (4): 285–304. http://dx.doi.org/10.1080/13645570110109115.

Canadian Press. 2003, "Fire Razes More Than 200 Homes in Kelowna, B.C." Retrieved 15 February 2004 (www.ctv.ca/servlet/ArticleNews/print?band=generic&archive=CTVNews&date=2).

Catano, James V. 2003. "Labored Language: Anxiety and Sadomasochism in Steel-Industry Tales of Masculinity." *Men and Masculinities* 6 (1): 3–30. http://dx.doi.org/10.1177/1097184X02250836.

CBC News. 2009a. "B.C. Interior Faces High Risk of Catastrophic Forest Fires." Retrieved 12 October 2010 (http://www.cbc.ca/news/canada/british-columbia/story/2009/05/22/bc-forest-fire-risk.html#socialcomments).

CBC News. 2009b. "Fighting Fire in the Forest: How Forest Blazes Start and Spread, and What Canadians Do to Fight Them." Retrieved 12 October 2010 (http://www.cbc.ca/canada/story/2009/06/17/f-forest-fires.html#ixzz12BYvW2r2).

CBC News. 2010. "B.C. Forest Fire Prevention Slammed by Experts: Author of Key Report Says Government Downplaying Risk." Retrieved 12 October 2010 (http://www.cbc.ca/news/canada/british-columbia/story/2010/06/07/bc-forest-fire-filman-report.html).

Charles, Maria, and David Grusky. 2004. *Occupational Ghettos.* Stanford, CA: Stanford University Press.

Charmaz, Kathy. 2000. "Grounded Theory: Objectivist and Constructivist Methods." In *Handbook of Qualitative Research*, ed. N.K. Denzin and Y.S. Lincoln, 509–35. Thousand Oaks, CA: Sage Publications.

Charmaz, Kathy. 2004. "Grounded Theory." In *Approaches to Qualitative Research*, ed. by S. Nagy Hesse-Biber and P. Leavy, 496–521. New York: Oxford University Press.

CHBC. 2003, "Fire Cools a Little." Retrieved 15 February 2004 (www.chbc. com.news/articles_files/6812/news_14_6812.shtml).

Chetkovich, Carol. 1997. *Real Heat: Gender and Race in the Urban Fire Service.* New Jersey: Rutgers University Press.

Childs, Merilyn, Michael Morris, and Valerie Ingham. 2004. "The Rise and Rise of Clean, White-Collar (Fire-Fighting) Work." *Disaster Prevention and Management* 13 (5): 409–14. http://dx.doi.org/10.1108/09653560410568534.

City of Kelowna. 2010, "Kelowna Fire Department." Retrieved 6 May 2010 (http://www.kelowna.ca/CM/page378.aspx).

Connell, R. 2009. *Gender.* Cambridge, UK: Polity.

Connell, R.W. 1987. *Gender and Power.* Stanford, CA: Stanford University Press.

Connell, R.W. 1995. *Masculinities.* Berkeley: University of California Press.

Connell, R.W. 2000a. *The Men and the Boys.* Berkeley: University of California Press.

Connell, R.W. 2000b. *Gender.* Malden, MA: Blackwell Publishers.

Connell, R.W. 2001. "Introduction and Overview." *Feminism & Psychology* 11 (1): 5–9. http://dx.doi.org/10.1177/0959353501011001001.

Connell, R.W. 2005. *Masculinities.* Berkeley: University of California Press.

Connell, R., and James Messerschmidt. 2005. "Hegemonic Masculinity: Rethinking the Concept." *Gender & Society* 19 (6): 829–59. http://dx.doi.org/10.1177/0891243205278639.

Cooper, Robyn. 1995. "The Fireman: Immaculate Manhood." *Journal of Popular Culture* 28 (4): 139–70. http://dx.doi.org/10.1111/j.0022-3840.1995.1395768.x.

Cornwell, Benjamin, Timothy J. Curry, and Kent Schwirian. 2003. "Revisiting Norton Long's Ecology of Games: A Network Approach." *City & Community* 2 (2): 121–42. http://dx.doi.org/10.1111/1540-6040.00044.

Cotterill, Pamela. 1992. "Interviewing Women: Issues of Friendship, Vulnerability, and Power." *Women's Studies International Forum* 15 (5-6): 593–606. http://dx.doi.org/10.1016/0277-5395(92)90061-Y.

Cox, R., B. Long, M. Jones, and R. Handler. 2008. "Sequestering of Suffering: Critical Discourse Analysis of Natural Disaster Media Coverage." *Journal of Health Psychology* 13(4): 469–80.

Curry, Timothy J. 1986. "A Visual Method of Studying Sports: The Photo-Elicitation Interview." *Sociology of Sport Journal* 3: 204–16.

Dalton, Susan, and Sarah Fenstermaker. 2002. "'Doing Gender' Differently: Institutional Change in Second-Parent Adoptions." In *Doing Gender, Doing Difference*, ed. S. Fenstermaker and C. West, 169–185. New York: Routledge.

Davis, Diane. 2005. "Reverberations: Mexico City's 1985 Earthquake and the Transformation of the Capital." In *The Resilient City: How Modern Cities*

Recover from Disaster, ed. L.J. Vale and T.J. Campanella, 255–80. New York: Oxford.

de Certeau, Michel. 1984. *The Practice of Everyday Life*. Berkeley: University of California Press.

de Wall, Alexander. 2008. Foreword. In *Capitalizing on Catastrophe, Globalization and the Environment*, ed. N. Gunewardena and M. Schuller, pp. ix–xiv. Lanham, MD: Altamira Press.

Dellinger, Kirsten. 2004. "Masculinities in 'Safe' and 'Embattled' Organizations: Accounting for Pornographic and Feminist Magazines." *Gender & Society* 18 (5): 545–66. http://dx.doi.org/10.1177/0891243204267401.

Denzin, Norman K., and Yvonna S. Lincoln. 2000. "Introduction: The Discipline and Practice of Qualitative Research." In *Handbook of Qualitative Research*, ed. N.K. Denzin and Y.S. Lincoln, 1–28. Thousand Oaks, CA: Sage Publications.

Desmond, Matthew. 2007. *On the Fireline*. Chicago: University of Chicago Press.

Deutsch, Francine. 2007. "Undoing Gender." *Gender & Society* 21 (1): 106–27. http://dx.doi.org/10.1177/0891243206293577.

DeVoss, Danielle. 2002. "Women's Porn Sites: Spaces of Fissure and Eruption, or, 'I'm a Little Bit of Everything.'" *Sexuality & Culture* 6 (3): 75–94. http://dx.doi.org/10.1007/BF02912229.

Drew, J. 2004. "Identity Crisis: Gender, Public Discourse, and 9/11." *Women & Language* 27: 71–7.

Dworkin, S.L., and F.L. Wachs. 2000. "The Morality/Manhood Paradox." in *Masculinities, Gender Relations, and Sport, vol. 13, Research on Men and Masculinities*, ed. J. McKay, M.A. Messner, and D.F. Sabo, 46–66. Thousand Oaks, CA: Sage.

Elliott, James, Timothy Haney, and Petrice Sams-Abiodun. 2010. "Limits to Social Capital: Comparing Network Assistance in Two New Orleans Neighborhoods Devastated by Hurricane Katrina." *Sociological Quarterly* 51 (4): 624–48. http://dx.doi.org/10.1111/j.1533-8525.2010.01186.x. Medline:20939128

Enarson, E. 1999a. "Violence Against Women in Disasters: A Study of Domestic Violence Programs in the US and Canada." *Violence Against Women* 5 (7): 742–68. http://dx.doi.org/10.1177/10778019922181464.

Enarson, E. 1999b. "Women and Housing Issues in Two U.S. Disasters: Case Studies from Hurricane Andrew and the Red River Valley Flood." *International Journal of Mass Emergencies and Disasters* 17:39–64.

Enarson, E. 2000. *Gender Equality, Work, and Disaster Reduction: Making the Connections*. Geneva: International Labor Organization.

Enarson, E. 2001. *"We Want Work": Rural Women in the Gujarat Drought and*

Earthquake. Boulder, CO: Natural Hazards Research and Applications Information Center, University of Colorado.

Enarson, E. 2006. *Women and Girls Last? Averting the Second Post-Katrina Disaster.* Brooklyn, NY: Social Science Research Council.

Enarson, E. 2012. *Women Confronting Natural Disaster: From Vulnerability to Resistance.* Boulder, CO: Lynne Rienner Publishers.

Enarson, E., and M. Fordham. 2001. "Lines That Divide, Ties That Bind: Race, Class, and Gender in Women's Flood Recovery in the U.S. and U.K." *Australian Journal of Emergency Management* 15:43–52.

Enarson, E., A. Fothergill, and L. Peek. 2006. "Gender and Disaster: Foundations and Directions." In *Handbook of Disaster Research*, ed. H. Rodríguez, E.L. Quarantelli, and R.R. Dynes, 130–46. New York: Springer.

Enarson, E., and B. Hearn Morrow. 1998a. "Women Will Rebuild: A Case Study of Feminist Response to Disaster." In *The Gendered Terrain of Disaster: Through Women's Eyes,* ed. E. Enarson and B. Hearn Morrow, 185–99. Westport, CT: Greenwood.

Enarson, Elaine, and Betty Hearn Morrow. 1998b. *The Gendered Terrain of Disaster: Through Women's Eyes.* Westport, CT: Praeger.

Enarson, Elaine. 1984. *Woods-Working Women.* Tuscaloosa: University of Alabama Press.

Enarson, Elaine, and Joseph Scanlon. 1999. "Gender Patterns in Flood Evacuation: A Case Study in Canada's Red River Valley." *Applied Behavioral Science Review* 7 (2): 103–24. http://dx.doi.org/10.1016/S1068-8595(00)80013-6.

Environment Canada. 2010. "Fujita Scale Rating the Severity of Tornadoes." Retrieved 15 December 2010 (http://www.ec.gc.ca/default. asp?lang=En&n=714D9AAE-1&news=697FC410-72B8-4598-A4CF-2B725FAE4D7A).

Eriksen, Christine, Nicholas Gill, and Lesley Head. 2010. "The Gendered Dimensions of Bushfire in Changing Rural Landscapes in Australia." *Journal of Rural Studies* 26 (4): 332–42. http://dx.doi.org/10.1016/j. jrurstud.2010.06.001.

Etkin, David. 1999. "Risk Transference and Related Trends: Driving Forces towards More Mega-Disasters." *Global Environmental Change Part B: Environmental Hazards* 1 (2): 69–75. http://dx.doi.org/10.1016/S1464-2867 (00)00002-4.

Filmon, Gary. 2004. "Firestorm 2003: Provincial Review." Government of British Columbia.

Finch, J. 1993. "It's Great to Have Someone to Talk To: Ethics and Politics of Interviewing Women." In *Social Research: Philosophy, Politics and Practice*, ed. M. Hammersley, 166–80. London: Sage.

Fine, Gary Alan. 1996. "Reputational Entrepreneurs and the Memory of Incompetence: Melting Supporters, Partisan Warriors, and Images of President Harding." *American Journal of Sociology* 101 (5): 1159–93. http://dx.doi.org/10.1086/230820.

Fine, Gary Alan, and Ryan White. 2002. "Creating Collective Attention in the Public Domain: Human Interest Narratives and the Rescue of Floyd Collins." *Social Forces* 81 (1): 57–85. http://dx.doi.org/10.1353/sof.2002.0046.

Flannigan, M., B. Amiro, K. Logan, B. Stocks, and B. Wotton. 2006. "Forest Fires and Climate Change in the 21st Century." *Mitigation and Adaptation Strategies for Global Change* 11 (4): 847–59. http://dx.doi.org/10.1007/s11027-005-9020-7.

Fletcher, Laurel, Eric Stover, and Harvey Weinstein. 2005. *After the Tsunami: Human Rights of Vulnerable Populations*. Berkeley: University of California, Human Rights Center.

Fontana, Andrea. 2001. "Postmodern Trends in Interviewing." In *Handbook of Interview Research*, ed. J.F. Gubrium and J.A. Holstein, 161–76. Thousand Oaks, CA: Sage.

Fordham, Maureen. 1999. "The Intersection of Gender and Social Class in Disaster: Balancing Resilience and Vulnerability." *International Journal of Mass Emergencies and Disasters* 17 (1): 15–37. Medline:12295202

Form, W.H., C.P. Loomis, R.A. Cliford, H.E. Moore, S. Nosov, G.P. Stone, and C.M. Westie. 1956. "The Persistence and Emergence of Social and Cultural Systems in Disasters." *American Sociological Review* 21 (2): 180–5. http://dx.doi.org/10.2307/2088519.

Fothergill, A. 1998. "Neglect of Gender in Disaster Work: An Overview of the Literature." In *The Gendered Terrain of Disaster: Through Women's Eyes*, ed. E. Enarson and B. Hearn Morrow, 11–25. Westport, CT: Praeger.

Fothergill, A. 1999. "An Exploratory Study of Woman Battering in the Grand Forks Flood Disaster." *International Journal of Mass Emergencies and Disasters* 17:79–98.

Fothergill, A., E.G. Maestas, and J.D. Darlington. 1999. "Race, Ethnicity and Disasters in the United States: A Review of the Literature." *Disasters* 23 (2): 156–73. http://dx.doi.org/10.1111/1467-7717.00111. Medline:10379098

Fothergill, Alice. 2004. *Heads Above Water*. Albany, NY: SUNY Press.

Foucault, M. 1980. *Power/Knowledge: Selected Interviews and Other Writings, 1972–1977*. New York: Pantheon Books.

Freake, Ross, and Don Plant. 2003. *Firestorm: The Summer BC Burned*. Toronto: McClelland & Stewart.

Fuchs Epstein, Cynthia. 1992. "Tinkerbells and Pinups: The Construction and Reconstruction of Gender Boundaries at Work." In *Cultivating Differences:*

Symbolic Boundaries and the Making of Inequality, ed. M. Lamont and M. Fournier, 232–56. Chicago: University of Chicago Press.

Gieryn, Thomas F. 1983. "Boundary Work and the Demarcation of Science from Non-Science: Strains and Interest in Professional Ideologies of Scientists." *American Sociological Review* 48 (6): 781–95. http://dx.doi.org/10.2307/2095325.

Gillett, N.P., A.J. Weaver, F.W. Zwiers, and M.D. Flannigan. 2004. "Detecting the Effect of Climate Change on Canadian Forest Fires." *Geophysical Research Letters* 31 (18), L18211: 1–4. http://dx.doi.org/10.1029/2004GL020876.

Girard, C., and W.G. Peacock. 1997. "Ethnicity and Segregation: Post-Hurricane Relocation." In *Hurricane Andrew: Ethnicity, Gender and the Sociology of Disasters*, ed. W.G. Peacock, B.H. Morrow, and H. Gladwin, 191–205. New York: Routledge.

Glaser, B.G. 1992. *Emergence vs. Forcing: Basics of Grounded Theory Analysis*. Mill Valley, CA: Sociology Press.

Glaser, B.G., and A.L. Strauss. 1967. *The Discovery of Grounded Theory: Strategies for Qualitative Research*. Chicago: Aldine.

Goffman, Erving. 1963. *Stigma: Notes on the Management of Spoiled Identity*. Englewood Cliffs, NJ: Prentice Hall.

Gramsci, A. 1971. *Selections from the Prison Notebooks*. Ed. Q. Hoare and G.N. Smith, trans. Q. Hoare and G.N. Smith. London: Wishart.

Grewal, I. 2003. "Transnational America: Race, Gender and Citizenship after 9/11." *Social Identities* 9 (4): 535–61. http://dx.doi.org/10.1080/1350463032000174669.

Harding, Sandra. 1987. "Introduction: Is There a Feminist Method?" In *Feminism and Methodology: Social Science Issues*, ed. S. Harding, 1–14. Bloomington, IN: Indiana University Press.

Harding, Sandra, and Kathryn Norberg. 2005. "New Feminist Approaches to Social Science Methodologies: An Introduction." *Signs: A Journal of Women in Culture & Society* 30 (4): 2009–15. http://dx.doi.org/10.1086/428420.

Harper, Douglas. 2000. "Reimagining Visual Methods." In *Handbook of Qualitative Methods*, ed. N.K. Denzin and Y.S. Lincoln, 717–32. Thousand Oaks, CA: Sage.

Hartmann, Heidi. 1981. "The Family as the Locus of Gender, Class, and Political Struggle: The Example of Housework." *Signs* 6 (3): 366–94. http://dx.doi.org/10.1086/493813.

Hearn Morrow, Betty. 1997. "Stretching the Bonds: The Families of Andrew." In *Hurricane Andrew: Ethnicity, Gender and the Sociology of Disasters*, ed. W.G. Peacock, B. Hearn Morrow, and H. Gladwin, 141–70. New York: Routledge.

Hearn Morrow, B., and W.G. Peacock. 1997. "Disasters and Social Change: Hurricane Andrew and the Reshaping of Miami?" In *Hurricane Andrew: Ethnicity, Gender, and the Sociology of Disasters*, ed. W.G. Peacock, B. Hearn Morrow, and H. Gladwin, 226–42. New York: Routledge.

Henkel, Kristin E., John F. Dovidio, and Samuel L. Gaertner. 2006. "Institutional Discrimination, Individual Racism, and Hurricane Katrina." *Analyses of Social Issues and Public Policy (ASAP)* 6 (1): 99–124. http://dx.doi.org/10.1111/j.1530-2415.2006.00106.x.

Heritage B.C. 2004, "Rebuilding the Myra Canyon Trestles." Retrieved 15 February 2004 (www.heritagebc.ca/n1_article4.htm).

Hertz, Rosanna. 1995. "Separate But Simultaneous Interviewing of Husbands and Wives: Making Sense of Their Stories." *Qualitative Inquiry* 1 (4): 429–51. http://dx.doi.org/10.1177/107780049500100404.

Hill Collins, Patricia. 2000. *Black Feminist Thought*. New York: Routledge.

Hoffman, E. 2007. "Open-Ended Interviews, Power, and Emotional Labor." *Journal of Contemporary Ethnography* 36 (3): 318–46. http://dx.doi.org/10.1177/0891241606293134.

Hoffman, S.M. 1998. "Eve and Adam among the Embers: Gender Patterns after the Oakland Berkeley Firestorm." In *The Gendered Terrain of Disaster: Through Women's Eyes*, ed. E. Enarson and B. Hearn Morrow, 55–62. Westport, CT: Praeger.

Hollander, J.A. 2002. "Resisting Vulnerability: The Social Construction of Gender in Interaction." *Social Problems* 49 (4): 474–96. http://dx.doi.org/10.1525/sp.2002.49.4.474.

Hondagneu-Sotelo, Pierrette, and Michael Messner. 1994. "Gender Displays and Men's Power: The 'New Man' and the Mexican Immigrant Man." In *Theorizing Masculinities*, ed. H. Brod and M. Kaufman, 200–18. Thousand Oaks, CA: Sage. http://dx.doi.org/10.4135/9781452243627.n11.

hooks, bell. 2000. *Feminist Theory: From Margin to Center*. Cambridge, MA: South End Press.

Horton, Lynn. 2012. "After the Earthquake: Gender Inequality and Transformation in Postdisaster Haiti." *Gender and Development* 20 (2): 295–308. http://dx.doi.org/10.1080/13552074.2012.693284.

Houchin Winfield, B. 2003. "The Press Response to the Corps of Discovery: The Making of Heroes in an Egalitarian Age." *Journalism & Mass Communication Quarterly* 80 (4): 866–83. http://dx.doi.org/10.1177/107769900308000408.

Houghton, Rosalind. 2009. "'Everything Became a Struggle, Absolute Struggle': Post-flood Increases in Domestic Violence in New Zealand." In *Women,*

Gender and Disaster: Global Issues and Initiatives, ed. E. Enarson and P.G. Dhar Chakrabarti, 99–111. Thousand Oaks, CA: Sage.

Howard, J.W., and L. Prividera. 2004. "Rescuing Patriarchy or Saving 'Jessica Lynch': The Rhetorical Construction of the American Woman Soldier." *Women & Language* 27:89–97.

Huggins, Martha, and Marie-Louise Glebbeek. 2003. "Women Studying Violent Male Institutions: Cross-Gendered Dynamics in Police Research on Secrecy and Danger." *Theoretical Criminology* 7 (3): 363–87. http://dx.doi.org/10.1177/13624806030073006.

Iacuone, David. 2005. "'Real Men Are Tough Guys': Hegemonic Masculinity and Safety in the Construction Industry." *Journal of Men's Studies* 13 (2): 247–66. http://dx.doi.org/10.3149/jms.1302.247.

Jeffreys, Sheila. 2007. "Double Jeopardy: Women, the US Military and the War in Iraq." *Women's Studies International Forum* 30 (1): 16–25. http://dx.doi.org/10.1016/j.wsif.2006.12.002.

Karanci, N.A., N. Alkan, B. Aksit, H. Sucuoglu, and E. Balta. 1999. "Gender Differences in Psychological Distress, Coping, Social Support and Related Variables Following the 1995 Dinar (Turkey) Earthquake." *North American Journal of Psychology* 1:189–204.

Kaufman, Michael. 2001. "The Construction of Masculinity and the Triad of Men's Violence." In *Men's Lives,* ed. M.S. Kimmel and M.A. Messner, 4–16. Needham Heights, MA: Allyn and Bacon.

Keller, Keith. 2002. *Wildfire Wars.* Madeira Park, BC: Harbour Publishing.

Kimmel, Michael S. 1994. "Masculinities as Homophobia: Fear, Shame, and Silence in the Construction of Gender Identity." In *Theorizing Masculinities,* ed. H. Brod and M. Kaufman, 119–41. Thousand Oaks, CA: Sage.

Kimmel, Michael S. 1996. *Manhood in America: A Cultural History.* New York: Free Press.

Kimmel, Michael S., Jeff Hearn, and R.W. Connell. 2005. *Handbook of Studies on Men and Masculinities.* Thousand Oaks, CA: Sage.

Kitzinger, Celia. 2009. "Doing Gender: A Conversation Analytic Perspective." *Gender & Society* 23 (1): 94–8. http://dx.doi.org/10.1177/0891243208326730.

Klatch, Rebecca. 1988. "The Methodological Problems of Studying a Politically Resistant Community." *Studies in Qualitative Methodology* 1:73–88.

Klinenberg, Eric. 2003. *Heat Wave: A Social Autopsy of Disaster in Chicago.* Chicago: University of Chicago Press.

Lamont, Michele. 2000. *The Dignity of Working Men: Morality and the Boundaries of Race, Class, and Immigration.* Cambridge, MA: Harvard University Press.

Langewiesche, W. 2002. *American Ground: Unbuilding the World Trade Center.* New York: North Point Press.

Larabee, Ann. 2000. *Decade of Disaster.* Urbana, Chicago: University of Illinois Press.

Legerski, Elizabeth Miklya, and Marie Cornwall. 2010. "Working-Class Job Loss, Gender, and the Negotiation of Household Labor." *Gender & Society* 24 (4): 447–74. http://dx.doi.org/10.1177/0891243210374600.

Lewis, J. and Ilan Kelman. 2012. "The Good, the Bad and the Ugly: Disaster Risk Reduction (DRR) versus Disaster Risk Creation (DRC)." *PLOS Currents Disasters*, June 21, edition 1. doi:10.1371/4f8d4eaec6af8..

Lewis, Sue. 2004. *Gender and Firefighting.* Melbourne, Australia: Swinburne University of Technology.

Liefbroer, Aart C., and Martine Corijn. 1999. "Who, What, Where, and When? Specifying the Impact of Educational Attainment and Labour Force Participation on Family Formation." *European Journal of Population / Revue europeenne de demographie* 15 (1): 45–75. http://dx.doi.org/10.1023/A:1006137104191. Medline:12159001

Lindell, Michael K. 2011. "Disaster Studies." *Sociopedia.isa*:1–18.

Logan, John. 2006. *The Impact of Katrina: Race and Class in Storm-Damaged Neighborhoods.* Providence, RI: Brown University.

Lois, Jennifer. 2003. *Heroic Efforts: The Emotional Culture of Search and Rescue Volunteers.* New York: New York University Press.

Lorber, Judith. 2002. "Heroes, Warriors, and Burqas: A Feminist Sociologist's Reflections on September 11." *Sociological Forum* 17 (3): 377–96. http://dx.doi.org/10.1023/A:1019674922707.

Lorber, Judith. 2005. *Breaking the Bowls: Degendering and Feminist Change.* New York: W.W. Norton.

Lovekamp, William E. 2010. "Promoting Empowerment: Social Change in Disasters." in *Social Vulnerability to Disasters*, ed. B. Phillips, D. Thomas, A. Fothergill, and L. Blinn-Pike, 367–81. Boca Raton, FL: CRC Press.

Luff, Donna. 1999. "Dialogue Across the Divides: 'Moments of Rapport' and Power in Feminist Research with Anti-feminist Women." *Sociology* 33:687–703.

Luft, Rachael. 2008. "Looking for Common Ground: Relief Work in Post-Katrina New Orleans as an American Parable of Race and Gender Violence." *National Women's Studies Association Journal* 20:5–31.

Luft, Rachael. 2011. "Disaster Patriarchy: An Intersectional Analysis of Post-Katrina Struggles for Community Power." Paper presented at the American Sociological Association Annual Meetings, 14–16 August. Las Vegas, NV.

Maier, Mark, and James Messerschmidt. 1998. "Commonalities, Conflicts, and Contradictions in Organizational Masculinities: Exploring the Gendered Genesis of the Challenger Disaster." *Canadian Review of Sociology and Anthropology. La Revue Canadienne de Sociologie et d'Anthropologie* 35 (3): 325–44. http://dx.doi.org/10.1111/j.1755-618X.1998.tb00726.x. Medline:11542273

Malin, Brenton J. 2005. *American Masculinity under Clinton: Popular Media and the Nineties Crisis of Masculinity.* New York: Peter Lang.

Martin, P.Y. 2001. "'Mobilizing Masculinities': Women's Experiences of Men at Work." *Organization* 8 (4): 587–618. http://dx.doi.org/10.1177/135050840184003.

Martin, Patricia Yancey. 2003. "'Said and Done' Versus 'Saying and Doing': Gendering Practices, Practicing Gender at Work." *Gender & Society* 17 (3): 342–66. http://dx.doi.org/10.1177/0891243203017003002.

Martin, Patricia Yancey, and David Collinson. 1999. "Gender and Sexuality in Organizations." In *Revisioning Gender: The Gender Lens*, ed. M.M. Ferree, J. Lorber, and B.B. Hess, 285–310. Thousand Oaks, CA: Sage.

Martin, Susan. 1994. "'Outsider Within' the Station House: The Impact of Race and Gender on Black Women Police." *Social Problems* 41 (3): 383–400. http://dx.doi.org/10.2307/3096969.

McCorkel, J., and K. Myers. 2003. "What Difference Does Difference Make? Position and Privilege in the Field." *Qualitative Sociology* 26 (2): 199–231. http://dx.doi.org/10.1023/A:1022967012774.

McDowell, Linda. 2009. *Working Bodies: Interactive Service Employment and Workplace Identities.* Chichester, UK: John Wiley & Sons.

Messerschmidt, James W. 1995. "Managing to Kill: Masculinities and the Space Shuttle *Challenger* Explosion." *Masculinities* 3:1–22.

Meyer, Stephen. 1999. "Work, Play, and Power: Masculine Culture on the Automotive Shop Floor; 1930–1960." *Men and Masculinities* 2 (2): 115–34. http://dx.doi.org/10.1177/1097184X99002002001.

Mileti, Dennis. 1999. *Disasters by Design.* Washington, DC.: Joseph Henry Press.

Miller, Jody, and Barry Glassner. 1997. "The 'Inside' and the 'Outside': Finding Realities in Interviews." In *Qualitative Research: Theory, Method and Practice*, ed. D. Silverman, 99–112. London: Sage.

Millett, Kate. 1969. *Sexual Politics.* New York: Doubleday.

Mishra, Prafulla. 2009. "Let's Share the Stage: Involving Men in Gender Inequality and Disaster Risk Reduction." In *Women, Gender and Disaster*, ed. E. Enarson and P.G. Dhar Chakrabarti, 29–39. Thousand Oaks, CA: Sage.

Mitchell, Juliet. 1974. *Psychoanalysis and Feminism.* New York: Vintage Books.

Mohanty, Chandra 1991. "Under Western Eyes: Feminist Scholarship and Colonial Discourses." In *Third World Women and the Politics of Feminism*, ed. C. Mohanty, A. Russo, and L. Torres, 51–80. Indianapolis: Indiana University Press.

Moloney, M., and S. Fenstermaker. 2002. Performance and Accomplishment: Reconciling Feminist Conceptions of Gender. In *Doing Gender, Doing Difference*, ed. S. Fenstermaker and C. West, 189–204. New York: Routledge.

Monaghan, Lee. 2002. "Hard Men, Shop Boys, and Others: Embodying Competence in a Masculinist Occupation." *Sociological Review* 50 (3): 334–55. http://dx.doi.org/10.1111/1467-954X.00386.

Morgan, David. 1992. *Discovering Men*. New York: Routledge.

Naples, Nancy. 2003. *Feminism and Method: Ethnography, Discourse Analysis, and Activist Research*. New York: Routledge.

Neal, D., and B. Phillips. 1990. "Female-Dominated Local Social Movement Organizations in Disaster-Threat Situations." In *Women and Social Protest*, ed. G. West and R. Blumberg, 243–55. New York: Oxford University Press.

Nentwich, Julia. 2008. "New Fathers and Mothers as Gender Troublemakers? Exploring Discursive Constructions of Heterosexual Parenthood and their Subversive Potential." *Feminism & Psychology* 18 (2): 207–30. http://dx.doi.org/10.1177/0959353507088591.

Netting, Nancy. 2010. "Marital Ideoscapes in 21st-century India: Creative Combinations of Love and Responsibility." *Journal of Family Issues* 31 (6): 707–26. http://dx.doi.org/10.1177/0192513X09357555.

Neumayer, Eric, and Thomas Plümper. 2007. "The Gendered Nature of Natural Disasters: The Impact of Catastrophic Events on the Gender Gap in Life Expectancy, 1981-2002." *Annals of the American Association of Geographers* 97 (3): 551–66. http://dx.doi.org/10.1111/j.1467-8306.2007.00563.x.

Nigg, J.M., and K. Tierney. 1993. "Disasters and Social Change: Consequences for Community Construct and Affect." *Annual Meeting of the American Sociological Association*, 13–17 August. Miami, Florida.

Oakley, Ann. 1981. "Interviewing Women: A Contradiction in Terms." In *Doing Feminist Research*, ed. H. Roberts, 30–61. London: Routledge and Kegan Paul.

Olesen, Virginia. 2000. "Feminisms and Qualitative Research At and Into the Millennium." In *Handbook of Qualitative Research*, ed. N.K. Denzin and Y.S. Lincoln, 215–55. Thousand Oaks, CA: Sage.

Ouellet, Lawrence. 1994. *Pedal to the Metal: The Work Lives of Truckers*. Philadelphia: Temple University Press.

Paap, Kris. 2006. *Working Construction*. Ithaca, NY: Cornell University Press.

Pacholok, Shelley. 2009. "Gendered Strategies of Self: Navigating Hierarchy and Contesting Masculinities." *Gender, Work and Organization* 16 (4): 471–500. http://dx.doi.org/10.1111/j.1468-0432.2009.00452.x.

Padavic, Irene. 1991. "The Re-creation of Gender in a Male Workplace." *Symbolic Interaction* 14 (3): 279–94. http://dx.doi.org/10.1525/si.1991.14.3.279.

Palinkas, Lawrence, Michael Downs, John Petterson, and John Russell. 1993. "Social, Cultural, and Psychological Impacts of the Exxon Valdez Oil Spill." *Human Organization* 52:1–13.

Peacock, W.G., and C. Girard. 1997. "Ethnic and Racial Inequalities in Disaster Damage and Insurance Settlements." In *Hurricane Andrew: Ethnicity, Gender, and the Sociology of Disaster*, ed. W.G. Peacock, B.H. Morrow, and H. Gladwin, 171–90. London: Routledge.

Pini, B. 2005. "Interviewing Men: Gender and the Collection and Interpretation of Qualitative Data." *Journal of Sociology* 41 (2): 201–16. http://dx.doi.org/10.1177/1440783305053238.

Plant, Don. 2003. "Hard Fought Battle." *Okanagan Sunday*, 24 August. Kelowna.

Pomerantz, S., D. Currie, and D. Kelly. 2004. "Sk8er Girls: Skateboarders, Girlhood, and Feminism in Motion." *Women's Studies International Forum* 27 (5-6): 547–57. http://dx.doi.org/10.1016/j.wsif.2004.09.009.

Poulsen, Chuck. 2003. "Unsung Heroes: Heavy Equipment Operators Put Their Lives on the Line Fighting the Okanagan Mountain Blaze, But Respect Has Been Hard to Find." *The Daily Courier*, 2 September. Kelowna.

Presser, Lois. 2005. "Negotiating Power and Narrative in Research: Implications for Feminist Methodology." *Signs: Journal of Women in Culture & Society* 30 (4): 2067–90. http://dx.doi.org/10.1086/428424.

Price, Linda. 2010. "'Doing It with Men': Feminist Research Practice and Patriarchal Inheritance Practices in Welsh Family Farming." *Gender, Place & Culture: A Journal of Feminist Geography* 17 (1): 81–97. http://dx.doi.org/10.1080/09663690903522438.

Prince, Samuel Henry. 1920. *Catastrophe and Social Change*. Columbia, NY: Political Science.

Projansky, S. 1998. "Girls Who Act like Women Who Fly: Jessica Dubroff as Cultural Troublemaker." *Signs: Journal of Women in Culture and Society* 23 (3): 771–808. http://dx.doi.org/10.1086/495288.

Prokos, Anastasia, and Irene Padavic. 2002. "'There Oughtta Be a Law Against Bitches': Masculinity Lessons in Police Academy Training." *Gender, Work and Organization* 9 (4): 439–59. http://dx.doi.org/10.1111/1468-0432.00168.

Pullen, Alison, and David Knights. 2007. "Editorial: Undoing Gender: Organizing and Disorganizing Performance." *Gender, Work and Organization* 14 (6): 505–11. http://dx.doi.org/10.1111/j.1468-0432.2007.00368.x.

Quam-Wickham. 1999. "Rereading Man's Conquest of Nature." *Men and Masculinities* 2:135–51.

Quarantelli, Enrico. 2005. "A Social Science Research Agenda for the Disasters of the 21st Century: Theoretical, Methodological and Empirical Issues and Their Professional Implementation." In *What Is a Disaster? New Answers to Old Questions*, ed. R.W. Perry and E.S. Quarantelli, 325–96. Philadelphia: Xlibris.

Quarantelli, Enrico L., Patrick Lagadec, and Arjen Boin. 2006. "A Heuristic Approach to Future Disasters and Crises: New, Old, and In-Between Types." In *Handbook of Disaster Research, Handbooks of Sociology and Social Research*, ed. H.B. Kaplan, H. Rodríguez, and E.L. Quarantelli, 16–41. Boston, MA: Springer.

Ranson, Gillian. 2005. "No Longer 'One of the Boys': Negotiations with Motherhood, as Prospect or Reality, among Women in Engineering." *Canadian Review of Sociology and Anthropology. La Revue Canadienne de Sociologie et d'Anthropologie* 42 (2): 145–66. http://dx.doi.org/10.1111/j.1755-618X.2005. tb02459.x.

Reinsch, Simone. 2009. "'A Part of Me Had Left': Learning from Women Farmers in Canada about Disaster Stress." In *Women, Gender, and Disaster: Global Issues and Initiatives*, ed. E.P.G.D. Chakrabarti, 152–64. Thousand Oaks, CA: Sage. http://dx.doi.org/10.4135/9788132108078.n12.

Reskin, Barbara. 1988. "Bringing the Men Back In: Sex Differentiation and the Devaluation of Women's Work." *Gender & Society* 2 (1): 58–81. http:// dx.doi.org/10.1177/089124388002001005.

Reskin, Barbara, and Patricia Roos. 1990. *Job Queues, Gender Queues*. Philadelphia: Temple University Press.

Rice, Carla. 2009. "Imagining the Other? Ethical Challenges of Researching and Writing Women's Embodied Lives." *Feminism & Psychology* 19 (2): 245–66. http://dx.doi.org/10.1177/0959353509102222.

Riessman, C.K. 2008. *Narrative Methods for the Human Sciences*. Thousand Oaks, CA: Sage.

Risman, Barbara J. 2009. "From Doing to Undoing: Gender as We Know It." *Gender & Society* 23 (1): 81–4. http://dx.doi.org/10.1177/0891243208326874.

Rodríguez, Havidán, Enrico L. Quarantelli, and R.R. Dynes. 2006. "Handbook of Disaster Research." In *Handbooks of Sociology and Social Research*. New York: Springer.

Ross, Karen. 2001. "Political Elites and the Pragmatic Paradigm: Notes from a Feminist Researcher—In the Field and out to Lunch." *International*

Journal of Social Research Methodology 4 (2): 155–66. http://dx.doi.
org/10.1080/13645570119027.

Rubin, Lillian. 2004. "The Approach-Avoidance Dance: Men, Women, and Intimacy." In *Men's Lives*, ed. M. Kimmel and M. Messner, 353–8. Boston: Allyn and Bacon.

Ruscher, Janet B. 2006. "Stranded by Katrina: Past and Present." *Analyses of Social Issues and Public Policy (ASAP)* 6 (1): 33–8. http://dx.doi.
org/10.1111/j.1530-2415.2006.00114.x.

Sandink, Dan. 2009. *The Resilience of the City of Kelowna: Exploring Mitigation Before, During and After the Okanagan Mountain Park Fire.* Toronto: Institute for Catastrophic Loss Reduction.

Sasson-Levy, Orna. 2002. "Constructing Identities at the Margins: Masculinities and Citizenship in the Israeli Army." *Sociological Quarterly* 43 (3): 357–83. http://dx.doi.org/10.1111/j.1533-8525.2002.tb00053.x.

Scanlon, Joseph. 1999. "Myths of Male and Military Superiority: Fictional Accounts of the 1917 Halifax Explosion." *English Studies in Canada* 24:1001–25.

Schuller, Mark. 2008. "Deconstructing the Disaster after the Disaster: Conceptualizing Disaster Capitalism." In *Capitalizing on Catastrophe*, ed. N. Gunewardena and M. Schuller, 17–27. Lanham, MD: Altamira Press.

Schwalbe, Michael, and Douglas Mason-Schrock. 1996. "Identity Work as Group Process." In *Advances in Group Processes*, vol. 13, ed. B. Markovsky, M. Lovaglia, and R. Simon, 113–47. Greenwich, CT: JAI Press.

Schwalbe, Michael, and Michelle Wolkomir. 2002. "Interviewing Men." In *Handbook of Interview Research: Context and Method*, ed. J. F. Gubrium and J.A. Holstein, 203–19. Thousand Oaks, CA: Sage.

Sered, Susan. 1999. "'Woman' as Symbol and Women as Agents." In *Revisioning Gender*, ed. M. Marx Ferree, J. Lorber, and B.B. Hess, 193–221. Thousand Oaks, CA: Sage.

Seymour, Ron. 2003. "Hot Stuff." *Daily Courier*, 29 August. Kelowna.

Sherman, R. 2005. "Producing the Superior Self: Strategic Comparison and Symbolic Boundaries among Luxury Hotel Workers." *Ethnography* 6 (2): 131–58.

Shibutani, Tamotsu. 1986. *Social Processes.* Berkeley: University of California Press.

Sinclair, Upton. 1935. *I, Candidate for Governor, and How I Got Licked.* New York: Ferrar and Rinehart.

Sjoberg, Gideon. 1962. "Disasters and Social Change." In *Man and Society in Disaster*, ed. G.W. Baker and D.W. Chapman, 356–84. New York: Basic Books.

Smith, Dorothy E. 1987. *The Everyday World as Problematic.* Boston: Northeastern University Press.

Snow, David, and Leon Anderson. 1987. "Identity Work among the Homeless: The Verbal Construction and Avowal of Personal Identities." *American Journal of Sociology* 92 (6): 1336–71. http://dx.doi.org/10.1086/228668.

Snow, David, and Leon Anderson. 1994. "The Problem of Identity Construction among the Homeless." In *Symbolic Interaction: An Introduction to Social Psychology*, ed. N. Herman and L. Reynolds, 239–58. Dix Hills, NY: General Hall.

Stake, Robert. 2000. "Case Studies." In *Handbook of Qualitative Research*, ed. N.K. Denzin and Y.S. Lincoln, 435–54. Thousand Oaks, CA: Sage.

Statistics Canada. 2006a. "Occupation: National Occupational Classification for Statistics 2006 (720), Class of Worker (6) and Sex (3) for the Labour Force 15 Years and Over of Canada, Provinces, Territories, Census Metropolitan Areas and Census Agglomerations; 2006 Census – 20% Sample Data. " Catalogue no. 97-559-XCB2006011. Ottawa: Statistics Canada.

Statistics Canada. 2006b. "Occupation: National Occupational Classification for Statistics 2006 (720C), Sex (3) and Selected Demographic, Cultural, Labour Force, Educational and Income Characteristics (273) for the Population 15 Years and Over of Canada, Provinces, Territories, Census Metropolitan Areas and Census Agglomerations; 2006 Census – 20% Sample Data."

Strauss, A. 1987. *Qualitative Analysis for Social Scientists*. Cambridge: Cambridge University Press. http://dx.doi.org/10.1017/CBO9780511557842

Strauss, A., and J. Corbin. 1998. *Basics of Qualitative Research: Techniques and Procedures for Developing Grounded Theory*. Thousand Oaks, CA: Sage.

Taylor, Verta. 1998. "Feminist Methodology in Social Movements Research." *Qualitative Sociology* 21 (4): 357–79. http://dx.doi.org/10.1023/A:1023376225654.

Thapar-Björkert, Suruchi, and Marsha Henry. 2004. "Reassessing the Research Relationship: Location, Position, and Power in Fieldwork Accounts." *International Journal of Social Research Methodology* 7 (5): 363–81. http://dx.doi.org/10.1080/1364557092000045294.

Thomas, Robyn, and Annette Davis. 2005. "What Have the Feminists Done for Us? Feminist Theory and Organizational Resistance." *Organization Articles* 12:711–40.

Thorne, Barrie. 2004. "'You Still Takin' Notes?' Fieldwork and Problems of Informed Consent." In *Approaches to Qualitative Research*, ed. S. Nagy Hesse-Biber and P. Leavy, 159–76. New York: Oxford University Press.

Tierney, K. 2007. "From the Margins to the Mainstream? Disaster Research at the Crossroads." *Annual Review of Sociology* 33 (1): 503–25. http://dx.doi.org/10.1146/annurev.soc.33.040406.131743.

Tobin, Graham, and Jane C. Ollenburger. 1999. "Women, Aging, and Post-Disaster Stress: Risk Factors for Psychological Morbidity." *International Journal of Mass Emergencies and Disasters* 17:65–78.

Tracy, Sarah, and Clifton Scott. 2006. "Sexuality, Masculinity, and Taint Management among Firefighters and Correctional Officers." *Management Communication Quarterly* 20 (1): 6–38. http://dx.doi.org/10.1177/0893318906287898.

U.S. Bureau of Labor Statistics. 2010. *Employed Persons by Detailed Occupation, Sex, Race, and Hispanic or Latino Ethnicity.* Ed. H.D. Survey. U.S. Bureau of Labor Statistics.

Vale, Lawrence J., and Thomas J. Campanella. 2005. "Introduction: The Cities Rise Again." In *The Resilient City: How Modern Cities Recover from Disaster,* ed. L.J. Vale and T.J. Campanella, 3–23. New York: Oxford.

Valocchi, Stephen. 2005. "Not Yet Queer Enough: The Lessons of Queer Theory for the Sociology of Gender and Sexuality." *Gender & Society* 19 (6): 750–70. http://dx.doi.org/10.1177/0891243205280294.

Van Willigen, Marieke. 2001. "Do Disasters Affect Individuals' Psychological Well-Being? An Over-Time Analysis of the Effect of Hurricane Floyd on Men and Women in Eastern North Carolina." *International Journal of Mass Emergencies and Disasters* 19:59–83.

Walby, Sylvia. 1989. "Theorising Patriarchy." *Sociology* 23 (2): 213–34. http://dx.doi.org/10.1177/0038038589023002004.

Waters, A. 2003. "Training and Experience Kept Trapped Firefighters Calm." *Capital News,* 27 August. Kelowna.

Weaver-Hightower, Marcus. 2002. "The Gender of Terror and Heroes? What Educators Might Teach about Men and Masculinity after September 11, 2001." *Teachers College Record,* ID no. 11012.

West, Candace, and Sarah Fenstermaker. 2002. "Power, Inequality, and the Accomplishment of Gender: An Ethnomethodological View." In *Doing Gender, Doing Difference: Inequality, Power, and Institutional Change,* ed. S. Fenstermaker and C. West, 41–54. New York: Routledge.

West, Candace, and Don H. Zimmerman. 1987. "Doing Gender." *Gender & Society* 1 (2): 125–51. http://dx.doi.org/10.1177/0891243287001002002.

West, Candace, and Don H. Zimmerman. 2009. "Accounting for Doing Gender." *Gender & Society* 23 (1): 112–22. http://dx.doi.org/10.1177/0891243208326529.

Williams, Christine. 1995. *Still a Man's World.* Berkeley: University of California Press.

Wisner, Ben. 2009. "The Grocer's Daughter and the Men in Suits: Who Exactly Capitalizes on Catastrophe? And Why the Question

Matters." *Capitalism, Nature, Socialism* 20 (3): 104–12. http://dx.doi.org/10.1080/10455750903215787.

Yoder, Janice, and Patricia Aniakudo. 1997. "'Outsider Within' The Firehouse: Subordination and Difference in the Social Interactions of African American Women Firefighters." *Gender & Society* 11 (3): 324–41. http://dx.doi.org/10.1177/089124397011003004.

Young, Iris M. 2005. "Socialist Feminist and the Limits of Dual Systems Theory." In *Theorizing Feminisms*, ed. E. Hackett and S. Haslanger, 490–501. Oxford University Press.

Index

Note: The abbreviation OMP refers to Okanagan Mountain Park.